AWS Certified A
Networking - Specialty

Practice Questions
Version 2

Document Control

Proposal Name	:	AWS – Advanced Networking - Specialty – Practice Questions
Document Version	:	2.0
Document Release Date	:	25th November 2019
Reference	:	ANS - C00

Feedback:

If you have any comments regarding the quality of this book, or otherwise alter it to better suit your needs, you can contact us through email at info@ipspecialist.net

Please make sure to include the book title and ISBN in your message.

About IPSpecialist

IPSPECIALIST LTD. IS COMMITTED TO EXCELLENCE AND DEDICATED TO YOUR SUCCESS.

Our philosophy is to treat our customers like family. We want you to succeed, and we are willing to do anything possible to help you make it happen. We have the proof to back up our claims. We strive to accelerate billions of careers with great courses, accessibility, and affordability. We believe that continuous learning and knowledge evolution are most important things to keep re-skilling and up-skilling the world.

Planning and creating a specific goal is where IPSpecialist helps. We can create a career track that suits your visions as well as develop the competencies you need to become a professional Network Engineer. We can also assist you with the execution and evaluation of proficiency level based on the career track you choose, as they are customized to fit your specific goals.

We help you STAND OUT from the crowd through our detailed IP training content packages.

Course Features:

❖ Self-Paced Learning
  • Learn at your own pace and in your own time
❖ Covers Complete Exam Blueprint
  • Prep-up for the exam with confidence
❖ Case Study Based Learning
  • Relate the content with real life scenarios
❖ Subscriptions that suits you
  • Get more and pay less with IPS Subscriptions
❖ Career Advisory Services
  • Let industry experts plan your career journey
❖ Virtual Labs to test your skills
  • With IPS vRacks, you can evaluate your exam preparations
❖ Practice Questions
  • Practice Questions to assess your preparation standards
❖ On Request Digital Certification
  • On request digital certification from IPSpecialist LTD.

About the Authors:

This book has been compiled with the help of multiple professional engineers. These engineers specialize in different fields e.g Networking, Security, Cloud, Big Data, IoT etc. Each engineer develops content in his/her specialized field that is compiled to form a comprehensive certification guide.

About the Technical Reviewers:

Nouman Ahmed Khan

AWS-Architect, CCDE, CCIEX5 (R&S, SP, Security, DC, Wireless), CISSP, CISA, CISM is a Solution Architect working with a major telecommunication provider in Qatar. He works with enterprises, mega-projects, and service providers to help them select the best-fit technology solutions. He also works as a consultant to understand customer business processes and to help select an appropriate technology strategy to support business goals. He has more than fourteen years of experience working in Pakistan/Middle-East & UK. He holds a Bachelor of Engineering Degree from NED University, Pakistan, and M.Sc. in Computer Networks from the UK.

Abubakar Saeed

Abubakar Saeed has more than twenty-five years of experience, Managing, Consulting, Designing, and Implementing large-scale technology projects, extensive experience heading ISP operations, solutions integration, heading Product Development, Presales, and Solution Design. Emphasizing on adhering to Project timelines and delivering as per customer expectations, he always leads the project in the right direction with his innovative ideas and excellent management.

Syed Hanif Wasti

Syed Hanif Wasti is a Computer Science Graduate working professionally as a Technical Content Developer. He is part of a team of professionals operating in the E-learning and digital education sector. He holds a Bachelor's Degree in Computer Sciences from PAF-KIET, Pakistan. He has completed training of MCP and CCNA. He has both technical knowledge and industry sounding information, which he uses efficiently in his career. He has also worked as a Database and Network administrator, having experience of software development.

Areeba Tanveer

Areeba Tanveer is working professionally as a Technical Content Developer. She holds Bachelor's of Engineering Degree in Telecommunication Engineering from NED University of Engineering and Technology. She previously worked as a project Engineer in Pakistan Telecommunication Company

4

Limited (PTCL). She has both technical knowledge and industry sounding information, which she uses effectively in her career.

Muhammad Yousuf

Muhammad Yousuf is a professional technical content writer. He is a Certified Ethical Hacker (v10) and Cisco Certified Network Associate in Routing and Switching, holding a Bachelor's Degree in Telecommunication Engineering from Sir Syed University of Engineering and Technology. He has both technical knowledge and industry sounding information, which he uses perfectly in his career.

Free Resources:

With each workbook you buy from Amazon, IPSpecialist offers free resources to our valuable customers.

Once you buy this book you will have to contact us at support@ipspecialist.net or tweet @ipspecialistoff to get this limited time offer without any extra charges.

Free Resources Include:

Exam Practice Questions in Quiz Simulation: With 500+ Q/A, IPSpecialist's Practice Questions is a concise collection of important topics to keep in mind. The questions are especially prepared following the exam blueprint to give you a clear understanding of what to expect from the certification exam. It goes further on to give answers with thorough explanations. In short, it is a perfect resource that helps you evaluate your preparation for the exam.

Career Report: This report is a step-by-step guide for a novice who wants to develop his/her career in the field of computer networks. It answers the following queries:

- What are the current scenarios and future prospects?
- Is this industry moving towards saturation or are new opportunities knocking at the door?
- What will the monetary benefits be?
- Why to get certified?
- How to plan and when will I complete the certifications if I start today?
- Is there any career track that I can follow to accomplish specialization level?

Furthermore, this guide provides a comprehensive career path towards being a specialist in the field of networking and also highlights the tracks needed to obtain certification.

Our Products

Technology Workbooks

IPSpecialist Technology workbooks are the ideal guides to developing the hands-on skills necessary to pass the exam. Our workbook covers official exam blueprint and explains the technology with real life case study based labs. The content covered in each workbook consists of individually focused technology topics presented in an easy-to-follow, goal-oriented, step-by-step approach. Every scenario features detailed breakdowns and thorough verifications to help you completely understand the task and associated technology.

We extensively use mind maps in our workbooks to visually explain the technology. Our workbooks have become a widely used tool to learn and remember the information effectively.

vRacks

Our highly scalable and innovative virtualized lab platforms let you practice the IP Specialist Technology Workbook at your own time and your own place as per your convenience.

Quick Reference Sheets

Our quick reference sheets are a concise bundling of condensed notes of the complete exam blueprint. It is an ideal handy document to help you remember the most important technology concepts related to the certification exam.

Practice Questions

IP Specialists' Practice Questions are dedicatedly designed in regards to the certification exam perspective. The collection of these questions from our technology workbooks are prepared keeping the exam blueprint in mind, covering not only important but necessary topics as well. It is an ideal document to practice and revise for your certification.

AWS Certifications

AWS Certifications are industry-recognized credentials that validate your technical cloud skills and expertise while assisting in your career growth. These are one of the most valuable IT certifications right now since AWS has established an overwhelming lead in the public cloud market. Even with the presence of several tough competitors such as Microsoft Azure, Google Cloud Engine, and Rackspace, AWS is by far the dominant public cloud platform today, with an astounding collection of proprietary services that continue to grow.

The two key reasons as to why AWS certifications are prevailing in the current cloud-oriented job market are:

- There is a dire need for skilled cloud engineers, developers, and architects – and the current shortage of experts is expected to continue into the foreseeable future
- AWS certifications stand out for their thoroughness, rigor, consistency, and appropriateness for critical cloud engineering positions

Value of AWS Certifications

AWS places equal emphasis on sound conceptual knowledge of its entire platform, as well as on hands-on experience with the AWS infrastructure and its many unique and complex components and services.

For Individuals

- Demonstrate your expertise to design, deploy, and operate highly available, cost-effective, and secure applications on AWS
- Gain recognition and visibility for your proven skills and proficiency with AWS
- Earn tangible benefits such as access to the AWS Certified LinkedIn Community, invite to AWS Certification Appreciation Receptions and Lounges, AWS Certification Practice Exam Voucher, Digital Badge for certification validation, AWS Certified Logo usage, access to AWS Certified Store
- Foster credibility with your employer and peers

For Employers

- Identify skilled professionals to lead IT initiatives with AWS technologies
- Reduce risks and costs to implement your workloads and projects on the AWS platform
- Increase customer satisfaction

Types of Certification

Role-Based Certifications:

- Foundational - Validates overall understanding of the AWS Cloud. It is a pre-requisite to achieving Specialty certification or an optional start towards Associate certification
- Associate - Technical role-based certifications. No pre-requisite required
- Professional - Highest level technical role-based certification. Relevant Associate certification required

Specialty Certifications:

- Validate advanced skills in specific technical areas
- Require one active role-based certification

About AWS – Certified Advanced Networking - Specialty Exam

Exam Questions	Multiple Choice and Multiple Answer
Time to Complete	170 minutes
Available Languages	English, Japanese, Korean, and Simplified Chinese
Practice Exam Fee	40 USD
Exam Fee	300 USD

The AWS Certified Advanced Networking – Specialty exam validates advanced technical skills and experience in designing and implementing AWS and hybrid IT network architectures at scale. This exam is intended for those individuals who perform complex networking tasks. Example concepts you should understand for this exam include:

- ➢ Design, develop, and deploy cloud-based solutions on AWS
- ➢ Implement core AWS services according to basic architecture best practices
- ➢ Design and maintain network architecture best practices
- ➢ Design and maintain network architecture for all AWS services
- ➢ Leverage tools to automate AWS networking tasks

Recommended AWS Knowledge

- One or more years of hands-on experience developing and maintaining an AWS based application
- In-depth knowledge of at least one high-level programming language
- Understanding of core AWS services, uses, and basic AWS architecture best practices
- Proficiency in developing, deploying, and debugging cloud-based applications using AWS
- Ability to use the AWS service APIs, AWS CLI, and SDKs to write applications
- Ability to identify key features of AWS services
- Understanding of the AWS shared responsibility model
- Understanding of application lifecycle management
- Ability to use a CI/CD pipeline to deploy applications on AWS
- Ability to use or interact with AWS services
- Ability to apply a basic understanding of cloud-native applications to write codes
- Ability to write codes using AWS security best practices (e.g. using IAM roles instead of using secret and access keys in the code)
- Ability to author, maintain, and debug code modules on AWS
- Proficiency writing code for server-less applications
- Understanding of the use of containers in the development process

	Domain	%
Domain 1	Design and implement hybrid IT network architectures at scale	23%
Domain 2	Design and implement AWS networks	29%
Domain 3	Automate AWS tasks	8%
Domain 4	Configure network integration with application services	15%
Domain 5	Design and implement for security and compliance	12%
Domain 6	Manage, Optimize, and Troubleshoot the Network	13%
Total		100%

Practice Questions

1- Your company wants to set up an AWS Direct Connect Connection and a VPN connection as a backup. In case the Direct Connect Connection fails, the traffic should be routed through the VPN line. What can be done for this scenario?

    A. In AWS Direct Connect, make the VPN the secondary device
    B. In AWS VPN, make AWS Direct Connect the primary device
    C. Enable bi-directional forwarding detection
    D. Enable BGP Routing

Answer: **C**

Explanation: Bi-directional Forwarding Detection is a network fault detection protocol that provides fast failure detection time, which then facilitates fast re-convergence time for dynamic routing protocols.

2- A company hosts its architecture in the US region and wants to duplicate this architecture in the Europe region. The company also wants to extend the application hosted on this architecture to a new region. How would the company ensure that users across the globe get the same experience?

    A. By creating a Classic Elastic Load Balancer to route traffic to both locations
    B. By creating a weighted Route53 policy to route the policy based on the weight for each location
    C. By creating an Application Elastic Load Balancer to route traffic to both locations
    D. By creating a geolocation Route53 policy to route the policy based on the location

Answer: **D**

Explanation: Geolocation routing enables you to route the traffic on basis of user's location. You have to choose resources that serve your traffic based on the geographic location of the user. For example, if queries from one region need to be routed to the ELB of other region, then we must select ELB as a resource.

3- You have 2 VPCs; VPC A and VPC B, which are both peered. You have configured the route table at VPC A so that traffic can flow from VPC A to VPC B. You try pinging an instance in VPC B from VPC A, but are unable to do so. You confirmed that NACLs and security groups have been configured properly. What could be the reason behind this failure?

    A. The VPCs have overlapping CIDR blocks
    B. Security Groups do not work in peered VPCs hence the requests will not work
    C. NACLs do not work in peered VPCs hence the requests will not work
    D. The route tables in VPC B have not been configured

Answer: **D**
Explanation: To send the traffic from one instance to another instance in peered VPCs, use IPV4 addressing. You just need to add the route to the route table that is associated with the subnet in which the instances reside. In order to communicate with the instance of VPC B, you need to add routes to allow traffic from instances of VPC A.

4- You work for an organization who has DirectConnect Connection and a backup VPN connection. After setting up both of these connections, the traffic flow prefers the VPN connection instead of DirectConnect Connection. You have pre-pended a longer AS path on the VPN connection, but even then, this connection is being preferred over the other one. Which of the following methods ensures that the Direct Connect Connection is used?

    A. Remove the prepended AS path
    B. Reconfigure the VPN as static a VPN instead of dynamic
    C. Increase the MED property on the VPN connection
    D. Advertise a less specific prefix on the VPN connection

Answer: **D**
Explanation: The route specified in the routing table is more specific for the VPN connection. The most specific route in your route table that matches the traffic determines how to route the traffic. It is better to configure a less specific route for VPN connections to ensure that it is not the preferred route which is taken.

5- An AWS admin team created AWS Workspace and noticed something strange. Users on the on-premises environment were not able to use the created workspace. What could be the issue?

    A. The AWS workspace has not been created properly. It needs to be recreated
    B. The ports on the company firewall are not open

C. The NACLs on the AWS workspace are not allowing incoming traffic

D. The security groups on AWS workspace are not allowing outbound traffic

Answer: **B**

Explanation: To connect to the workspace, the network on which AWS WorkSpace clients are connected must have certain ports open to the IP address ranges for the multiple AWS services on firewall.

6- Your company plans to deploy EC2 instances across multiple regions. These instances will make calls to S3. You are trying to understand the data transfer cost which is incurred in such implementations. Which one of the following is not charged by AWS?

A. Amazon EC2 in eu-west-1 to Amazon S3 in us-east-1

B. Your on-premises data center to Amazon S3 in us-east-1

C. Amazon EC2 in eu-west-1 to your on-premises data center

D. Amazon S3 in us-east-1 to Amazon EC2 in EU-west-1

Answer: **B**

Explanation: The data transferred through the internet to AWS is not charged beacsue there are no charges for data transfer in. There are no charges for the data transferred between S3 buckets in same region or from S3 to any AWS service.

7- A company needs to send a large amount of data that is to be ingested in S3. This has to be done on a daily basis, and the data transfer needs to be encrypted. The data transfer line needs to be dependable and of low-latency. How can you make this happen?

A. By using an AWS VPN Managed Connection

B. By using an AWS Direct Connect Connection

C. By using an AWS Managed VPN over AWS Direct Connect Connection

D. By using AWS Direct Connect over an AWS Managed VPN

Answer: **C**

Explanation: You can utilize AWS VPN over AWS Direct Connect Connection to get all the features of low latency and encrypted connection.

8- Your company plans to use Route53 as DNS provider. They want to ensure that the company domain name points to an existing CloudFront Distribution. How would you achieve this?

A. By creating an ALIAS record, which points to the CloudFront Distribution

B. By creating a host record, which points to the CloudFront Distribution

C. By creating a CNAME record, which points to the CloudFront Distribution

D. By creating a non-alias record, which points to the CloudFront Distribution

Answer: **A**

Explanation: Ordinary Route 53 records are standard DNS records, and alias records provide a Route 53 specific extension to DNS functionality. Instead of an IP address or a DNS name, alias records contain a pointer to CloudFront Distribution. When Route 53 receives a DNS query that matches the name and type in alias record, Route 53 follows the pointer and responds with the desired values.

9- Your team is planning on hosting an application in AWS using MySQL database that is hosted on EC2 instance. It is anticipated that the disk performance might take a hit due to input/output activity. How can you ensure baseline performance with low latency database?

A. By using an instance with Enhanced Networking enabled

B. By using EBS IOPS volumes

C. By using the EFS file system

D. By using Amazon S3 for storage

Answer: **B**

Explanation: Amazon EBS enables you to create and attach storage volumes to Amazon EC2. You can create a file system on top of these volumes and once it is attached, run a database, or otherwise use block storage. Amazon EBS offers a range of options to optimize storage and workload performance. These options have been divided into two main categories:

- SSD-backed storages for transaction workloads, such as databases and boot volumes (performance is mainly IOPS-related)
- HDD-backed storages for hard-hitting workloads, such as MapReduce and MB/s processing

In SSD backed volumes, Provisioned IOPS SSD has highest performance for latency sensitive data.

10- An IT security department deployed a firewall on AWS EC2 instance. It ensured that all traffic from certain applications needs to move through the firewalls. How would the department achieve maximum performance in this scenario? (Choose 2)

A. By considering to use an Amazon Linux AMI only

B. By using the underlying instance types

C. By using Driver support for the Intel Virtual Function and Elastic Network Adapter (ENA)

D. By considering to use NACLs

Answer: B

Explanation: Higher instance type provides higher performance, so choose higher instance type. Enhanced Networking is used to provide better networking support. In EC2, Enhanced Networking feature is provided via ENA or Intel 82599 VF interface, which uses the Intel ixgbevf drivers.

11- A team sets up a testing environment using VPC and EC2 instances, and an application is hosted on these instances. Some of the housekeeping scripts are developed using AWS Lambda that needs to delete the files created by EC2 instance on their respective EBS volume. What initial configuration needs to be put first?

A. Ensure to use the –vpc-config when creating the AWS Lambda function

B. Ensure to use the –vpc-config when creating the EC2 instance

C. Ensure the VPC has a route entry to the Lambda function

D. Ensure an internet gateway is attached to the VPC

Answer: A

Explanation: AWS Lambda runs the function code securely within the VPC by default. To enable Lambda function to access your resource inside the private VPC, you must provide the additional VPC specific configuration information that includes VPC subnet IDs and security group IDs.

12- An organization plans to set up a management network on the AWS VPC. The organization is trying to secure the web server on a single EC2 instance in such a way that it allows the internet traffic as well as the backend management traffic. The organization wants to make sure that the backend management interface can receive the SSH traffic only from the selected IP range. The internet has a web server, which has an IP address that can receive traffic from all of the internet IPs. How can this be achieved by running a web server on a single instance?

A. It is not possible to have 2 IP addresses for a single instance

B. The organization should create two network interfaces, one for internet traffic and the other for the backend traffic

C. The organization should create 2 EC2 instances as it is not possible with one EC2 instance

D. It is not possible

Answer: **B**

Explanation: You can attach 2 Elastic Network Interfaces (ENIs) to the instance. One ENI is used to accept internet traffic, and the other is used to interact with your instance inside the private subnet.

13- A company is planning to set up an AWS Direct Connect Connection to access the resources in AWS through its on-premises data center. It is estimating the involved cost. Which of the following should be taken into account for this? (Choose 3)

A. A number of port hours consumed
B. Data transfer into AWS Direct Connect
C. Data transfer from an S3 bucket via a public VIF
D. Data transfer from a VPC via a private VIF

Answer: **A, C, & D**

Explanation: In AWS Direct Connect, you have to pay for the port hours and data transfer out. Incoming data is not charged.

14- A company plans to use CloudFront Distribution, and the origin will be an S3 bucket. It wants to ensure that the users cannot access the objects in the S3 bucket through the public URL of the bucket object. How can this be achieved?

A. By creating a CloudFront origin identity that has access via the bucket policy
B. By placing an IAM policy, which ensures that users cannot access the objects
C. By creating a CloudFront origin identity that has access via the IAM policy
D. By creating a separate IAM user that has access via the bucket policy

Answer: **A**

Explanation: When you create or update a distribution, you can add an Origin Access Identity and update the bucket policy. Through this, you provide permission to Origin Access Identity to access the objects from the bucket. For such type of access use bucket policy not IAM policy. By using this technique on behalf of a user that requires your objects via CloudFront, CloudFront can access objects in a bucket. Users can not use Amazon S3 URLs to access objects.

15- Your team is using an application that is hosted in two different regions in AWS. EC2 instances are performing replication process in between the applications across the region

with respective Elastic IPs. The current MTU is 1500, and there is a need to increase the throughput for the replication traffic. How can you achieve this?

    A. By creating a VPN tunnel between the two VPCs and increasing the MTU on the instances
    B. By increasing the MTU on the instances
    C. By installing the Enhanced Networking Modules in the instances
    D. This is not possible

Answer: **D**

Explanation: You are already working at the maximum MTUs. 1500 MTUs are available for the traversing of traffic via the internet. If you are in VPC, then you can use Jumbo frames. Jumbo frames allow more than 1500 bytes by increasing the payload size per packet.

16- You are hosting an application on Amazon Linux EC2 instance, and you are required to reduce the amount of time it takes to process the EC2 instance packets. Which one of the following can be used to accomplish this?

    A. An instance that supports the Windows AMI
    B. Data Plane Development Kit
    C. Jumbo frames for packet transmission
    D. An MTU of 12,000

Answer: **B**

Explanation: Data Plane Development Kit consists of libraries which are used to accelerate packet process workload running on a wide variety of CPU architectures.

17- A team has created a CloudFormation template. The template consists of the creation of a virtual private gateway, customer gateway, and a VPN connection based on the created artifacts. During the creation, an error keeps occurring and the routes are not added because of the Virtual Private Gateway resource. How can you resolve this issue?

    A. By changing the order of the creation of resources in the template
    B. By adding a DependsOn attribute to the VPGW on the route table
    C. By adding a DependsOn attribute to the route table entry on the VPGW
    D. By adding a customer resource to the template for the route table entry

Answer: **C**

Explanation: By using DependsOn attribute, you can specify the creation of a specific resource that follows another resource. After adding a DependsOn attribute to a resource, resources can only be created after the creation of the resource that is specified in the DependsOn attribute.

18- You need to design a TLS/SSL solution that requires HTTP clients to be authenticated by the web server with the use of client certificate authentication. You also want the solution to be resilient. How will you configure the web server's infrastructure? (Choose 2)

    A. By configuring ELB with TCP listeners on TCP/443 and placing the web servers behind it

    B. By configuring the web servers using EIPs then placing the web server in the Route53 recordset and configuring health checks against all web servers

    C. By configuring ELB with HTTPS listeners and placing the web servers behind it

    D. By configuring the web servers as the origins for a CloudFront Distribution and using common SSL certificates on CloudFront Distribution

Answer: **A & B**

Explanation: A load balancer can be created that uses the SSL/TSL protocols for encrypted connections. This feature enables traffic encryption between the load balancer and the client who initiates the HTTP session, and the connection between the load balancer and EC2 instance. ELBs cannot currently support customer-side authentication. For successful two-way SSL authentication, the SSL / TLS certificate is required. So, the other way is by configuring the web servers with Elastic IP address. Web servers are the endpoint for traffic. Let DNS server Route 53 send requests in Round Robin fashion to those web servers.

19- You are creating an AWS Direct Connect Connection between the on-premises data center and AWS partner location. You have to make sure that the network supports the connection. What should be done to maintain the connection? (Choose 3)

    A. The network must have support for 802.1Q VLAN

    B. The network device must support BGP

    C. The network device must support static routing

    D. Auto-negotiation for the port must be disabled for the network device

Answer: **A, B, & D**

Explanation: These are some requirements for AWS Direct Connect Connection. Auto-negotiation for the port must be disabled. Port speed and full duplex mood must be configured manually. 802.1 Q VLAN must be supported throughout the network, including intermediate

devices. Optionally, you can configure Bi-directional Forwarding Detection (BFD) on your network.

20- A company has setup CloudFront Distribution that is using EC2 instances as the origin. There is a need to ensure that cookies are monitored in the requests. Depending on cookies, multiple sites must be relayed back to the users. How can this requirement be fulfilled?

    A. By using multiple origins
    B. By using Lambda at the edge
    C. By using proxy protocol
    D. By using RTMP distribution

Answer: **B**
Explanation: A Lambda function can inspect cookies and re-write URLs so that users see a different version of the site for A/B testing. A Lambda function can generate HTTP code when CloudFront viewer request or origin request events occur. A function may inspect headers or authorization tokens and insert the header before CloudFront sends a request to the source for accessing a specific content.

21- A database is running on a large instance type. It is noticed that the packets are getting lost and the instance is not delivering request as desired. A test was done initially to check the capacity of the server. At that time, the database server was capable of taking the load. What could be the issue?

    A. The right AMI was not chosen for the underlying instance
    B. The instance was using accumulated network credits during the testing phase
    C. There are internal database errors that are causing the timeouts
    D. The instance is not using a VPN tunnel for communication

Answer: **C**
Explanation: The database is not performing well under the load and hence giving the TCP errors.

22- A company wants to deploy an application on AWS. There is a requirement to provide high availability and low latency between the underlying instances that support the application. From the following options, which method is not suitable for the requirement?

    A. Deploying instances across multiple availability zones
    B. Enabling Enhanced Networking on the instances

C. Using a network Load Balancer in front of the instances

D. Placing the instances in a cluster placement group

Answer: D

Explanation: Launching an instance in the spread placement group reduces the risk of failure that might occur when the instances share the same underlying hardware. If the instance is placed in the cluster placement group, then they need to be placed in a single availability zone. This would not meet the requirement of high availability.

A distributed placement group can cover several Availability Zones, and you can run up to seven instances per group per available zone.

23- A CloudFormation template creates a VPC and a subnet with a CIDR block of 10.0.0.0/16. Another subnet in the VPC is created with a CIDR block of 10.0.1.0/24. What will happen when you try to deploy the template?

    A. The template will give an error during the design stage

    B. The template will give a deployment error when creating the subnet and leave the VPC as created

    C. The template will give a deployment error, and all resources will be rolled back

    D. The template will deploy successfully

Answer: C

Explanation: The template deployment will fail, and all resources will be rolled back due to overlapping CIDR blocks.

24- Your company plans to set up an Active Directory Domain server in VPC, and resources inside other VPCs will need to access domain server for authentication and DNS routing. What would be the core implementation for such a design? (Choose 2)

    A. Considering a Hub and Spoke model VPC design

    B. Making use of VPC peering

    C. Considering a transit VPC design

    D. Making use of a VPN connection

Answer: A & B

Explanation: VPC peering (partially meshed network) approach enables customers to connect VPCs as required and is a common policy for clients with a central VPC with shared resources. In the VPC sharing scenarium, customers use VPC peering in a hub and spoke formation to

connect selected VPCs to the central VPC. The central VPCs may require complete or partial access to the VPCs, and the VPCs may require complete or partial access to the central VPC. In this, central VPC hub and other VPCs that are spoke to are present. This is best suited when you have shared services that need to be shared across multiple other VPCs.

25- Your company has set up an AWS Direct Connect connection with the help of an AWS partner, and the customer gateway is on the on-premises data center. You need to inform the operations department when the Direct Connect connection goes down. How can you achieve this?

    A. By using the AWS Direct Connect tunnel logging facility to check for any failures

    B. By using CloudWatch metrics to check for the state of the tunnel

    C. By using Cloud Watch logs to check for the state of the tunnel

    D. You will anyway be notified if the AWS Direct Connect Connection is down

Answer: **B**

Explanation:

The AWS Direct Connect Connection has a metric available in CloudWatch called Connection State. You can design or set the alarm whenever the connection state is down.

26- A company's management is planning on using the AWS CloudFront to speed up the distribution of content to users from S3 bucket. The company wants its user to get the ideal response when they request objects from CloudFront. How would the user get content from the CloudFront?

    A. If a user requests an object, only when the entire object is available, it is sent to the user. This is to ensure a correct user experience

    B. If a user requests an object, the user is directed to the origin location for retrieval of the object

    C. As soon as the first byte arrives from the origin, CloudFront begins to forward the files to the user

    D. Amazon CloudFront will respond with an HTTP 404 error

Answer: **C**

Explanation: CloudFront checks its cache for the requested file in the edge location. If the files are in cache, CloudFront returns them to the user. If they are not in the cache;

- CloudFront compares the request with the specification in user's distribution and forwards the request for the files to the applicable origin server for the corresponding file type
- The origin servers will redirect the files to the edge of CloudFront

Once the first byte comes from the source, CloudFront will start to send the documents to the user. CloudFront also provides cache files for when someone requests the cache at edge.

27- A company is using an EC2 instance for handling the voice-related traffic. A custom application is launched on Linux based instance. How can higher bandwidth be achieved for this application?

   A. By enabling Enhanced Networking on the instance
   B. By using a Network Load Balancer in front of the EC2 instance
   C. By using a Placement Group for the EC2 instance
   D. By using an Application Load Balancer in front of the EC2 instance

Answer: **A**

Explanation: The best choice is to use Enhanced Networking. It uses single I/O virtualization to provide high-performance networking capabilities on supported instance types. Enhanced Networking provides higher bandwidth, higher packet per second performance and consists of low latencies.

28- A company is planning on hosting its VPN server in AWS. This will be hosted on EC2 instance and will use software from the AWS Market place. You have to ensure the optimal performance of the underlying VPN server. Which of the following would you consider? (Choose 2)

   A. Ensuring that the instance is using EBS optimized volumes
   B. Ensuring that the instance is using Enhanced Networking
   C. Understanding the packet limitations in the infrastructure
   D. Using a Network Load Balancer for scaling

Answer: **B & C**

Explanation: The instance must use Enhanced Networking for better network throughput. Conduct all the necessary test initially on the system to understand the overall performance of the system and check their limitations.

29- You are setting up a network architecture for a company. The architecture consists of an application that will exchange a lot of information and needs a high bandwidth consideration. There will be some B2B customers that may access the application in separate tenants. What would be your consideration in this design?

    A. Using a virtual private gateway for each customer as this will provide the least latency

    B. Using AWS Direct Connect for each customer. This will depend on the availability of an AWS partner in that location of the customer

    C. Using AWS VPN for each customer. This will depend on the availability of an AWS partner in that location of the customer

    D. Allowing each customer to connect via the internet then setting up the right security groups and NACLs for the application

Answer: **B**

Explanation: AWS Direct Connect offers a dedicated and high bandwidth connection to each customer, but AWS partner must be available to ensure a connection from the customer's location.

30- You have an on-premises application that needs to access S3. Some of the key requirements for the applications are high bandwidth, low jitter, and high availability. Which options would you consider in the design?

    A. Using the public internet to access the S3 service

    B. Using AWS Direct Connect with a private VIF

    C. Using AWS Direct Connect with a public VIF

    D. Using an IPSec VPN connection to a Virtual private Gateway

Answer: **C**

Explanation: AWS Direct Connect makes it easy to create a dedicated network connection from your premises to AWS. By using Direct Connect, you can establish private connectivity between AWS and your data center, office or co-location environment. Via AWS Direct Connect, your network expenses can often be lowered, bandwidth throughput increased and network experience can be more compatible than Internet-based links. With Public VIF, it is used in order to access public services like S3.

31- A company plans to set up a VPN connection between a VPC hosted on AWS and its on-premises data center. You have to ensure that the VPN connection is highly available and the cost is kept minimum. How can you fulfil this requirement?

    A. By creating 2 VPN connections for high availability
    B. By creating an additional Direct Connect Connection
    C. By creating an additional VPC peering connection
    D. VPN connections already have high availability

Answer: **A**

Explanation: To provide redundancy and high availability, each Virtual Private Gateway has two VPN endpoints. To make VPN connection highly available, you can use redundant customer gateways and dynamic routing for automatic failover between AWS and customer VPC endpoints.

32- You are trying out an AWS VPN managed connection, and you have created the VPN to connect to your on-premises location. Earlier, you were using an internet gateway. You added the VPN connection to your routing table and enabled propagation. The routing table is shown below:

Destination	Target
10.0.0.0/16	Local
172.31.0.0/24	Vgw-1a2b3c4d (propagated)
172.31.0.0/24	Igw-11aa22bb

Based on the above table, which of the following statement is true?
    A. Traffic destined for 172.31.0.0/24 will go through the virtual private gateway
    B. Traffic destined for 172.31.0.0/24 will go through the Internet gateway
    C. Traffic destined for 172.31.0.0/24 will go through the Local router
    D. This is not possible; you cannot have two routes with the same destination

Answer: **B**
Explanation: As per the given route table, there is static route to an internet gateway which we must add manually and propagate the route to VGW. The destination for both routes are

172.31.0.0./24. Because of the priotiy of the static route, all the traffic will be routed to the internet gateway.

33- To host a set of high-performance computing nodes that are used to process images and videos. Which of the following should be considered during implementation? (Choose 2)

  A. Using t2 large instances
  B. Using c5 instances
  C. Placing the instances in a placement group
  D. Using Linux based AMIs

Answer: **B & C**

Explanation: High-performance computing workloads on AWS run on virtual servers known as instances enabled by EC2. Amazon EC2 provides resizable capacity in the cloud, and it is offered in wide range of instance types, so you can choose the one that is optimized for your workload. C5 is used for compute intensive workload like video and image processing, genomics processing, metrology etc. You can also use placement group in order to meet the requirement of your workload.

34- A production team had earlier established a VPC with CIDR block of 192.168.0.0/16. Instances were launched in the VPC. Now, it is required to ensure that the instances have an address space for 10.0.0.0/16. How can this be achieved?

  A. By adding a new address space to the VPC then ensuring that the instances use the new address space
  B. By creating a new VPC with the address block of 10.0.0.0/16 and migrating all of the instances to the new VPC
  C. By changing the address block of the VPC from 192.168.0.0/16 to 10.0.0.0/16. All of the instances will now use the new address space
  D. By launching NAT instance and ensuring that the instance performs network address translation onto the CIDR range of 10.0.0.0/16

Answer: **B**

Explanation: When you are trying to add different CIDR blocks in an existing VPC from the main CIDR block, you will get an error. Hence, for different address blocks, you need to create a new VPC.

35- A company plans to host an application on EC2 instances. You are required to set up end-to-end encryption for the data to ensure that the application is HIPAA complaint. Which of the given options is suitable for this scenario?

    A. Ensuring that the traffic is encrypted using KMS
    B. Setting up a VPN connection between the EC2 instance and the internet
    C. Setting up a Direct Connect Connection between the EC2 instance and the internet
    D. Using SSL to encrypt all the data at the application layer

Answer: **D**

Explanation: For end-to-end encryption of data, use an SSL certificate that can be mapped to the application. The other options are not valid as KMS is used for encryption at rest. VPN does not encrypt the traffic and Direct Connect is not suitable for encryption.

36- Your company has an AWS Direct Connect Connection from a VPC to an on-premises location. In case Direct Connect connection fails, which of the following can be used for backup? (Choose 2)

    A. There is no need to configure it, as AWS will fall back to a secondary Direct Connect connection as per their SLA
    B. A secondary Direct Connect connection
    C. A VPN connection
    D. A peering connection

Answer: **B & C**

Explanation: If a second AWS Direct Connect connection is created, traffic will automatically failover to connect to the second connection. When configuring the links, we suggest that you allow Bi-directional Forwarding Detection (BFD) to guarantee quick detection and failure. If you have set up an IPsec VPN backup link instead, any VPC traffic will automatically failover to connect to a VPN. Public resources traffic to/from Amazon S3 will be routed via the internet.

37- To maintain version control and achieve automation in an organization's application, you have been requested to use CloudFormation. The environment will consist of several networking components and application services. How can you design the template?

A. By creating separate templates based on functionality and creating nested stacks with CloudFormation
B. By using CloudFormation custom resources to handle dependencies between stacks
C. By creating multiple templates in one CloudFormation stack
D. By combining all resources into one template for version control and automation

Answer: **A**

Explanation: Create a separate stack for networking so it can be managed separately. For managing multiple components custom resource is not the right option to choose and also managing multiple templates in one stack is not possible.

38- A company wants to set up a VPN connection between its AWS VPC and on-premises data center. The company needs to setup GRE VPN as the standard routing protocol. How can this requirement be fulfilled?

A. By using AWS managed VPN connections
B. By using Cloud Hub VPN to create a secure VPN connection
C. By creating an EC2 instance and then using software from the AWS market place
D. By using AWS Direct Connect

Answer: **C**

Explanation: The normal AWS VPN managed connection cannot be used; there is a requirement to use custom routing protocols instead of IPSec. You have to decide on creating an EC2 instance and using a custom VPN software from AWS market place for this GRE VPN requirement.

39- A company plans on creating a private hosted zone in AWS. You have to make sure that on-premises devices can reach the resources defined in the private hosted zone. With least efforts, how can you implement this?

A. By considering to use simple AD for resolving DNS requests
B. By converting the private hosted zone to a public one
C. By creating an EC2 instance and installing a DNS resolver
D. By creating an EC2 instance and AD domain services

Answer: **A**

Explanation: Simple AD transmits DNS requests to the IP address of the DNS servers provided for your VPC by Amazon. These DNS servers solve names and set up in the privately hosted zones of your Route 53. You can now resolve DNS requests into the private hosted zones by pointing your on-site computers to your Simple AD.

40-You have created a set of EC2 Linux based instances in the placement group and selected instances with Enhanced Networking enabled. Now, you have to ensure that a maximum number of packets can be sent across the network interface. How can you achieve this?

    A. By setting the Network Access Control List to the maximum network packet size
    B. By setting the Placement Group settings to the maximum network packet size
    C. By changing the MTU setting on the Ethernet interface for each instance
    D. By changing the Jumbo Frame setting on the Ethernet interface for each instance

Answer: **C**

Explanation: Some of the instances are configured to use jumbo frames while some are configured to use standard size frames. It depends on whether you want to use the jumbo frame for network traffic within your VPC, or you may want to use standard frames for internet traffic. The MTU (Maximum Transmission Unit) of a network connection is the byte size of the biggest allowable packet to pass through the connection. Ethernet frames can be produced in various formats and the standard Ethernet v2 frame format is the most common format. It promotes 1,500 MTUs, the biggest Ethernet packet size on the Internet. The highest instance MTU supported relies on the type of instances. Amazon EC2 instance models support 1,500 MTU and support 9,001 MTU or jumbo frames with many type of instances. So as per your requirements, set the MTU size.

41- For the VPC in AWS account, your architect team recommends the following requirements:
- A shared service VPC that would be able to provide services to other VPCs
- Hosted VPCs that can be accessible by customers
- The hosted VPC should also be able to interact with shared service VPC

Which of the following can be considered as a suitable design for this implementation? (Choose 2)

    A. Ensure that a virtual private link is available for accessing the shared service VPC
    B. Use VPC peering between the shared service VPC and other VPCs

C. Put the shared service VPC as public. Ensure the right security measures are in place for accessing the shared services

D. Create a VPN between each VPC. Ensure the virtual private gateway is in place for the other VPCs

Answer: **A & C**

Explanation: One choice is to build a VPC-private link to access the AWS-shared VPC services. You can create and configure your own application in the VPC as an AWS-enabled Private Link service. Other AWS managers can connect from their VPC to your endpoint service via the interface VPC endpoint. You are the service provider and service customers are the AWS directors who make links to your service.

You can also create a public VPC as well but right security measures are also need to be taken.

42- A company plans to use Route53 for managing Blue/Green deployment. It has already set up 80% 20% for a new deployment. How would you make sure to terminate sending traffic to the older setup, once all testing is done?

A. By deleting the weighted resource record

B. By changing the resource record to a simple routing policy

C. By changing the resource record weight to 100

D. By changing the resource record weight to 0

Answer: **D**

Explanation: Set weight equivalent to 0 for disabling routing to a resource. If you set the weight for all records in the group at zero, traffic is likely to be routed to all resources, equally.

43- You have 9 EC2 instances running in a Placement Group. All these nine instances were initially launched at the same time and are working as expected. You decided to add two more instances in the group, but after this attempt, you receive a capacity error. How can you fix this issue?

A. By making a new Placement group and launching the new instances in the new group. Also, by making sure the Placement Groups are in the same subnet

B. By stopping and restarting the instances in the Placement Group and then trying to launch again

C. By requesting a capacity increase from AWS as you are initially limited to 10 instances per Placement Group

D. By making sure all the instances are the same size and then trying the launch again

Answer: **B**

Explanation: If you get an "InsufficientInstanceCapacity" error when you try to launch an instance or restart a stopped instance, it means that AWS does not currently have enough available On-Demand capacity to successfully complete your request. To resolve this issue, you can do the following:

- Wait a couple of minutes then request again; the capability can change often
- Send a new request with a small amount of instances. For example, if you are requesting 15 instances for a single request, try making three requests for five instead of 15 requests for one instance
- Submit new request without defining an AZ
- Request for new instance with different instance type
- Stop and restart the instance in placement group and then try to launch again

44-A team is using a NAT instance on Linux EC2 instance. The private subnet has a route added for 0.0.0.0/0 for the NAT instance, which is being used to download updates from the internet in the private subnet for instances. However, the IT admin complains for the slow response time. How can this issue be rectified? (Choose 2)

A. By adding another NAT instance and another route for 0.0.0.0/0 to the new NAT instance

B. By replacing the NAT instance with a NAT gateway

C. By upgrading the NAT instance to a larger instance type

D. By moving the NAT instance to the private subnet as so it is closer to the other instances

Answer: **B & C**

Explanation: The bandwidth capability of the NAT instance depends on the instance type. NAT gateway in each availability zone is implemented with high redundancy and can scale up to 45 Gbps. You may also have another option like; to upgrade the instance size of NAT instance.

45-A company plans to deploy an EC2 instance that is used to route VPN traffic to an on-premises data center. What is the responsibility of AWS in this case?

    A. Ensuring high availability of the EC2 instance
    B. Ensuring high availability of the VPN connection
    C. Ensuring the health of the underlying physical host
    D. Ensuring the configuration of the IPSec protocol

Answer: **C**

Explanation: AWS is responsible for ensuring the underlying physical host of the EC2 instance. The customer is planning to use the AWS managed connection rather than adopting a custom VPN connection. Hence, the customer is responsible for all the underlying configuration, while AWS is responsible for health of physical host.

46- For designing your company's online shopping application, you need a VPC running on EC2 instance behind the Application Load Balancer. The instances run on Auto Scaling Group across multiple availability zones. The application tier must read and write data to the customer-managed database cluster. There is no access to the database from the internet, but cluster must be capable of obtaining software patches from the internet. Which VPC design meet these requirements?

    A. Public subnets for both the application tier and the database cluster
    B. Public subnets for the application tier, and private subnets for the database cluster and NAT instance
    C. Public subnets for the application tier and NAT gateway, and private subnets for the database cluster
    D. Public subnets for the application tier, and private subnets for the database cluster and NAT gateway

Answer: **C**

Explanation: You could use a Network Address Translation (NAT) gateway to enable instances in a private subnet to connect with the internet or different AWS offerings with denying initiation of connection to the internet for those instances. You are charged for creating and using a NAT gateway for your account as NAT gateway's hourly utilization and statistics processing are charged. Amazon EC2 charges for data switch are additionally applied.

47- You are currently managing a web server hosted on the EC2 instance with public IP addresses; the IP addresses are mapped on the domain name. An urgent management activity needs to be done on the server, which has to restart after the activity. Now, the web application hosted

on the EC2 instances is no more accessible through the domain name configured earlier. What could be the reason?

- A. The Route53 hosted zone needs to be restarted
- B. The network interfaces need to initialize again
- C. The public IP addresses need to be associated with the ENI again
- D. The public IP addresses have changed after the instance was stopped and started

Answer: **D**

Explanation: By default, the public IP address of an EC2 instance is released after the instance is stopped or started. Hence, the earlier IP address that was mapped on the domain name is no more valid now.

48-You have created a VPC connection containing 3 VPCs, VPC A, VPC B, and VPC C. There is a VPC peering connection between VPC A and VPC B and separate peering connection between VPC B and VPC C. Which statement is true in regards with VPC peering arrangement?

- A. Instances launched in VPC A can reach instances in VPC C
- B. Instances launched in VPC A can reach instances in VPC C if the right routing entries are present
- C. Instances launched in VPC A can reach instances in VPC C if the right security group rules are present for the instances
- D. Instances launched in VPC A can reach instances in VPC C via a proxy instance in VPC B

Answer: **D**

Explanation: Transitive peering is not allowed, so requests are forward through proxy instances.

49-A set of instances is setup in AWS VPC. You have to make sure that instances present in the VPC receive hostname from AWS DNS. You have configured the enableDNSHostName attribute set to true for VPC. But the instances are not receiving hostname when they are launched. What could be the main reason for this?

- A. The Auto-Assign public IP is not set for the subnet in which the instance is launched
- B. The EnablezDNS support is not set to true for the VPC

C. You need to configure a Route53 private hosted zone first

D. You need to configure a Route53 public hosted zone first

Answer: B

Explanation: To obtain the hostname, you have to set both values (DNS hostname and DNS support) to true. If both values are set to true, a public hostname will be given to your instance. The DNS server supplied by Amazon can sort out the private DNS hostname given by Amazon.

50- You enabled an Amazon Redshift cluster and started loading the tables in the cluster using COPY command. The internet is utilized while the data is being copied and you want to change this as so no internet is required. How should you perform this?

A. By ensuring the NACLs are set on the subnets hosting the Redshift cluster

B. By ensuring Enhanced VPC routing is enabled for the Redshift cluster

C. By ensuring the Security Groups are set on the EC2 instances hosting the Redshift cluster

D. By ensuring the routing table points to a VPN instead of the internet gateway

Answer: B

Explanation: Amazon Redshift Enhanced VPC routing should be implemented when you do not want to use internet while copying data. Amazon Redshift forces all the COPY and UNLOAD traffic between the cluster and the data repositories through the Amazon VPC rather than internet via Enhanced VPC routing.

51- A team is trying to ingest 1 TB of data using a large instance in Amazon S3. Enhanced Networking is enabled on this instance but the data ingestion process is running very slow. How can this issue be rectified?

A. By using an AWS Direct Connect Connection between S3 and the instance

B. By creating a VPC endpoint from the instance to S3

C. By using two instances and splitting the ingestion of data

D. By creating a VPN connection from the instance to S3

Answer: C

Explanation: Uploading a single large object is not feasible, and hence it is possible to split the object across multiple instances and carry out the data ingestion process.

52- You are using a Window server 2012 on your on-premises location as the customer gateway, and have set up the VPN connection and Virtual Private Gateway. You have also set up the VPN configuration on Window server 2012. But the tunnel's status is showing that it is down in AWS console. What needs to be done to make sure that the tunnel is in the UP state?

    A. Issue a ping command request from the Windows server 2012 device

    B. From the AWS console, choose the VPN connection, choose Action-> Bring Up tunnel

    C. From the AWS console, choose the Virtual private gateway, choose Action -> Bring up tunnel

    D. Ensure that the BGP routing protocol is set up on the Windows server 2012 device

Answer: **A**

Explanation: To check if the VPN connection is working properly, launch an instance into the VPC and make sure that it does not have an internet connection. After launching the instance, ping its private IP address from the Windows server. The VPN tunnel comes up, when the traffic is generated from the customer gateway; the ping command also launches the VPN connection.

53- An organization had a set of resources that were hosted in AWS. It acquired another company and hosted its resources in AWS. Now, it wants the resources in the VPC of the parent company to access the resources in the VPC of the child company. How can this be achieved with minimum cost?

    A. By using a Direct Connect Connection with a private VIF

    B. By establishing a NAT gateway to establish communication across VPCs

    C. By using a VPN connection to peer both VPCs

    D. By using VPC peering to peer both VPCs

Answer: **D**

Explanation: VPC Peering allows you to connect VPCs. The VPCs can be in different regions in different AWS accounts.

54- A company sets up a connection between its on-premises data center to AWS. Now, it wants the traffic to get directed to Data Center 2 when the primary connection to Data Center 1 goes down. What should be done during the implementation phase? (Choose 2)

A. Ensure that static routes are in place. Ensure the routes are changed in case of a failover
B. Ensure Data Center 2 advertises less specific routes
C. Make use of AS-path prepending
D. Make use of AWS Direct Connect as well

Answer: **B & C**

Explanation: Specific routes: Both Customer Gateway 1 and Customer Gateway 2 advertise a summary route of 10.0.0/15. Moreover, Customer Gateway 1 advertises 10.0.0.0/16 and Customer Gateway 2 advertises 10.1.0.0/16. AWS uses more special routes to transmit traffic to the appropriate data center. If the more specific road becomes temporarily unavailable, then reverse it to the other data center after the summarized route.

AS Path Prepending: With this approach, Customer Gateway 1 as well as Customer Gateway 2 advertise 10.0.0.0/16 and 10.1.0.0/16. Customer Gateway 1, however, it utilizes AS-path prepending to decrease this path preference by advertising 10.1.0.0/16 network. Customer Gateway 2 uses AS-paths prepending similarly, to make this path less preferred by advertising 10.0.0.0/16 network. AWS uses the preferred paths for sending traffic to the relevant data center, and if needed, it will fail back to the other data center following the less preferred routes.

55- You know that a VPC consists of public and private subnets, and private subnets use NAT instances to download updates from the internet. The instances are trying to download the updates from the server that works on port 8090, but they are unable to reach the external servers for updates. What might be the reasons? (Choose 2)

A. The NAT instance is blocking traffic on port 8090
B. The inbound NACL is blocking traffic on port 8090
C. The inbound Security Groups are blocking traffic on port 8090
D. The remote server firewall is blocking traffic

Answer: **A & D**

Explanation: The NAT instance is blocking outbound traffic at port 8090, which means it is not allowing the traffic to flow outward and the remote server is also blocking the traffic from the instances.

56- You want to set up a CloudFront distribution in AWS, and also use the AWS Certification Manager along with the CloudFront. While, setting up Cloud Front, you notice that the ACM

Certificate, which you created at an earlier stage to associate with the distribution, is not seen. What is the main issue?

    A. You have not uploaded or created the certificate in the right region

    B. You need to upload the certificate directly to CloudFront after the distribution is created

    C. You need to ensure that a CNAME record is created in Route53 first

    D. You need to ensure that an ALIAS record is created in Route53 first

Answer: **A**

Explanation: Like most AWS sources, certificate in ACM is regional resource. To use a certificate with Elastic Load Balancing for the identical Fully Qualified Domain called (FQDN) or set of FQDNs in multiple AWS regions, you have to request or import a certificate for each region. To apply an ACM certificate with Amazon CloudFront, you should request or import the certificates inside the US East (N. Virginia) region. ACM certificates in this place, that are associated with a CloudFront distribution, are allotted to all of the geographic locations configured for that distribution. You cannot copy certificates among regions.

57- A company's production team created a multi-AZ Amazon RDS instance. The application is communicating with the instance through custom DNS A record, but the primary database failed, and the application could no longer connect with the RDS. How can this issue be prevented in future?

    A. By ensuring that the application is using the Amazon RDS hostname

    B. By ensuring that the primary database is quickly swapped with the secondary one

    C. By ensuring that the application is using the IP address of primary database instance

    D. By ensuring that the application is using the IP address of secondary database instance

Answer: **A**

Explanation: The application must be connected through the Amazon RDS hostname. In case of primary instance failure, this will automatically be swapped with the secondary instance in the backend by AWS.

58- A web application is hosted on the set of EC2 instances behind an Application Load Balancer. All the security groups and NACLs are working with tight security. Which of the following

steps should be taken to ensure the blocking of DDoS attacks from the malicious IP addresses?

    A. Consider placing the WAF service in front of the Application Load Balancer

    B. Consider placing an AWS Private Link service in front of the Application Load Balancer

    C. Consider placing an AWS Shield Service in front of the Application Load Balancer

    D. Consider adding more restrictive rules to the network ACLs

Answer: **A**

Explanation: AWS WAF is a web application that monitors the web requests that are forwarded to CloudFront distribution or an Application Load Balancer. It can also be used to block or allow the request as specified according to the conditions (such as IP addresses from where the requests originate) or the values in the requests.

59- A company has the following Direct Connect and VPN connections:

- Site A: VPN 10.1.0.0/24 AS 65000 65000
- Site B: VPN 10.1.0.253/30 AS 65000
- Site C: Direct Connect 10.0.0.0/8 AS 65000
- Site D: Direct Connect 10.0.0.0/16 AS 65000 65000 65000

You want to connect to the IP address 10.1.0.254. Which of the following route will you choose?

    A. Site A

    B. Site B

    C. Site C

    D. Site D

Answer: **B**

Explanation: AWS uses the most specific route in the routing table that matches with your traffic; meaning the path with longest prefix. So, site B has the longest prefix, therefore this path will be chosen to connect to an IP address 10.1.0.254.

60- A company has EC2 instances hosted on AWS, and these instances have hosted an application. Currently, the application is facing some issues. You have to analyze the network packets to find out which type of errors are occurring. Which of the following helps in resolving this issue?

A. Using VPC flow logs
B. Using a network monitoring tool provided by an AWS partner
C. Using another instance. Setting up a port to "promiscuous mode" and sniffing the traffic to analyze the packets
D. Using CloudWatch metric

Answer: **B**

Explanation: Here, you need to sniff the packets, so the best approach is to use the network monitoring tool provided by an AWS partner. Multiple members of AWS Partner Network give virtual firewall devices, which can be used as an interactive portal for inbound, or outbound network traffic. Additional application filtering, deep packet inspection, IPS / IDS and network threat security characteristics are provided by the firewall devices.

61- You are transferring the data through public IPs of the EC2 instances. For this, you have launched a couple of EC2 instances in separate subnets. Both instances are located in the same AZ, and they are in the us-east-1 region. What are the data transfer charges?

A. There is no data transfer charge for instances in the same region
B. There is no data transfer charge for instances in the same AZ
C. There will be a data transfer charge of $0.01/GB
D. There is no data transfer charge for the internet

Answer: **C**

Explanation: The data transfer in or out of multiple AWS service across a VPC peering connection within the same AWS region is charged 0.01$ per GB. These services include: Amazon EC2, Amazon RDS, Amazon Redshift, Amazon DynamoDB Accelerator, and Amazon ElastiCache instances or Elastic Network Interface.

62- A company has a set of instances hosted in a private subnet, and these instances need to make the call to Amazon S3. You have set up the endpoint but you are still not capable of accessing S3 bucket from the private subnet instances. What is the reason behind this? (Choose 2)

A. The company might be using an interface instead of a gateway for accessing the S3 service
B. The prefix for the endpoint is not attached to the route table
C. The prefix for the endpoint is not attached to the Security Group
D. The endpoint is attached to the wrong VPC

Answer: **B & D**

Explanation: The prefix for the gateway endpoint needs to be added in the routing table. So even after setting up the endpoint, you are still unable to access S3 bucket from private VPC because may be the endpoint is attached to the wrong VPC or prefix for endpoint is not attached to route table.

63- You recently set up a web and database tier in a VPC and hosted an application. While testing the application, you are not able to access the home page of the app, and you have verified the security groups. Which one of the following helps you in diagnosing the issue?

    A. AWS Trusted Advisor, to see what can be done
    B. VPC Flow Logs, to diagnose the traffic
    C. AWS WAF, to analyze the traffic
    D. AWS Guard Duty, to analyze the traffic

Answer: **B**

Explanation: VPC Flow Logs capture the network flow information for a VPC, subnets or network interfaces and store it in CloudWatch Logs. This can help customers in troubleshooting the issues. This can be used as the security tool to monitor the traffic that reaches their instances.

64- There is an architecture that consists of the following components:
- Primary and secondary infrastructure that are hosted on AWS
- Both of the infrastructures consist of ELB, Auto-Scaling and EC2 resources

In case, the primary infrastructure goes down, how should Route53 be configured to ensure proper failover?
    A. By configuring a primary routing policy
    B. By configuring a weighted routing policy
    C. By configuring a multi-answer routing policy
    D. By configuring a failover routing policy

Answer: **D**

Explanation: You can create active-passive failover configuration by using failover record. You can create primary and secondary failover records that have the same type and name, and you associate a health check along with each failover.

65- A company has a set of AWS Direct Connect Connection. It wants to aggregate the bandwidth for these connections so that large amount of data can be sent across the pipes. A decision is made to set up a Link Aggregation Group. Which factors must be kept in mind while setting the LAG group? (Choose 2)

    A. The existing AWS Direct Connect connections have the same bandwidth
    B. A VPN connection is in place to attach to the LAG group
    C. All AWS Direct Connect connections terminate at the same AWS endpoints
    D. All AWS Direct Connect connections terminate at the different AWS endpoints

Answer: **A & C**

Explanation: All connections in the LAG must have the same bandwidth, and the following bandwidths should support 1Gbps and 10Gbps. You can have a maximum of 4 connections in LAG, and all the connections in LAG must terminate at the same AWS endpoint.

66- A company has a department that sets its AWS account, which is not a part of the consolidating billing process for the company. The company has setup AWS Direct Connect connection to a VPC through Private VIF and is downloading data in VPC from EC2 instance. How would the charges come across?

    A. The company would be charged for data transfer out via the internet gateway
    B. The company would be charged for data transfer out via AWS Direct Connect
    C. The department would be charged for data transfer out via the internet gateway
    D. The department would be charged for data transfer out via AWS Direct Connect

Answer: **D**

Explanation: Since the department uses the account irrespective of the company, they would get charged for data transfer out, depending on AWS region and Direct Connect connection location.

67- A Lambda function is designed to probe for the event on EC2 instances. After the probe, the Lambda function is required to send requests to the SQS queue. How can you achieve this? (Choose 2)

    A. By creating a NAT instance in the VPC

    B. By ensuring that the VPC configuration is added to the Lambda function

    C. By ensuring that the Lambda function details are added to the VPC configuration

    D. By ensuring that IPV6 is enabled for the subnet hosting the Lambda function

Answer: **A & B**

Explanation: Lambda function uses the VPC information that you provided to set ENIs that allow your Lambda function to access AWS resources. Each ENI is assigned a private IP address. You can configure NAT instance inside your VPC or you can configure VPC NAT gateway.

68-You are working as an AWS administrator in a company, and have setup classic load balancer and EC2 instances for an application. You have configured HTTP listener by default security policies, but the security department mentioned that the security policy defined for the load balancer does not meet the regulations defined for the policy. What changes would you make to achieve the requirements of the IT Security department?

    A. Create a new SSL and associate it with the underlying EC2 instances

    B. Create a new SSL and associate it with the underlying Classic Load Balancer

    C. Create a Custom Security policy and associate it with the EC2 instance

    D. Create a Custom Security policy and associate it with the Classic Load Balancer

Answer: **D**

Explanation: Create a Custom security policy in line with the IT department and then associate it with Classic Load Balancer.

69-Your company hosts an application that consists of NGINX web server hosted behind an Application Load Balancer. You need to make sure that you restrict access to the content hosted on the web server in some locations. How can you achieve this?

    A. By using the NGINX logs to get the web server variable and then using the IP address to restrict content via CloudFront geo-restrictions

    B. By using the ELB logs to create a blacklist for restrictions

    C. By using the IP addresses in the X-forwarded for HTTP header and then restricting content via CloudFront geo-restrictions

    D. By using the ELB itself to restrict content via geo-restrictions

Answer: **C**

Explanation: You can use geo-restriction, also known as geo-blocking, to prevent users in specific geographic locations from accessing content that you are distributing through a CloudFront web distribution. To use geo-restriction, you have two options:

Use the CloudFront geo-restrict feature: Use this selection to limit access to all the documents that are associated with distribution and to limit access at the country level.

Use a 3rd-party geolocation carrier: Use this feature to restrict the right of entry to a subset of the documents that might be associated with a distribution or to restrict access at a finer granularity than the country level.

70- A company has multiple remote branch offices that need to connect with your AWS VPC. What can you use achieve this connectivity in an easy manner?

  A. VPN Cloud Hub
  B. AWS Direct Connect with a Public VIF
  C. AWS Direct Connect with a Private VIF
  D. VPC Peering

Answer: **A**

Explanation: If you have multiple VPN connections, you can provide communication between the sites using VPN CloudHub. This enables remote communications between the sites, not just in VPN.

71- A private subnet is defined in a VPC. You have to make sure that instances must reach to a server through the internet and the response from the external server must be replayed back to the private server on the pre-defined ports. How can you achieve this?

  A. By moving the EC2 instance to a public subnet
  B. By installing Squid Proxy on an EC2 instance
  C. By using a NAT gateway in the Public Subnet
  D. By using the NAT gateway in the Private subnet

Answer: **B**

Explanation: You cannot use a NAT gateway because port forwarding is the key requirement. So, you need to use the customized NAT instance.

72- You decided to use VPC flow logs to monitor the traffic to EC2 instance on your VPC. Which of the following types of traffic will not be monitored by VPC flow logs? (Choose 2)

    A. Instances that have multiple ENIs
    B. Traffic that flows to Amazon DNS servers
    C. Instances that have Elastic IPs assigned to the ENI
    D. Requests for instance metadata

Answer: **B & D**

Explanation: The Flow Logs will not include any of the following traffic:

- Traffic to Amazon DNS servers, including queries for private hosted zones
- Traffic to licenses provided by Amazon for Windows license activation
- Requests for instance metadata
- DHCP requests or responses

73- A company plans to open AWS Direct Connect Connection, and wants to make sure that its router has the desired capabilities to support this connection. Which of the following is going to be supported by the routers? (Choose 3)

    A. Single Mode Fiber
    B. 1 Gbps Copper Connection
    C. 802.1Q VLAN
    D. BGP and BGP AD5 Authentication
    E. 802.1ad

Answer: **A, C, & D**

Explanation:

- The network must use Single Mode Fiber with a 1000BASE-LX (1310nm) transceiver for 1 Gigabit Ethernet or a 10GBASE-LR (1310nm) transceiver for 10 Gigabit Ethernet
- Auto-negotiation for the port must be disabled. Port speed and full-duplex mode must be configured manually
- 802.1Q VLAN encapsulation must be supported across the entire connection, including intermediate devices
- Your device must support the Border Gateway Protocol (BGP) and BGP MD5 authentication

- (Optional) You can configure Bidirectional Forwarding Detection (BFD) on your network. Asynchronous BFD is automatically enabled for AWS Direct Connect virtual interfaces but does not take effect until you configure it on your router

74- An EC2 instance is responsible for processing videos and audios. Now, it is required to make sure that the EC2 instance has maximum performance when it comes to network packet processing. How can this be obtained? (Choose 2)

  A. By ensuring that the instance supports single root I/O virtualization
  B. By ensuring that the MTU is set to 9001 on the instance
  C. By ensuring that the MTU is set to 9001 for the VPC
  D. By choosing a t2 medium instance type

Answer: **A & B**

Explanation: Enhanced Networking uses single root I/O virtualization, which is used to provide high network performance capabilities to all supported instance types. SR-IOV is a method of device virtualization that provides high I/O performance and less CPU utilization.

75- A company has a 3-tier application that consists of a Web, Application, and database tier. The application is based on REST-full services. The company also has EC2 instances and auto-scaling groups for web and application tiers. Now, there is a need to add high availability to the tier, and each tier must be scaled independently. What should be the architecture?

  A. Create an Application Load Balancer and add separate target groups for the Web and Application tier
  B. Create an Application Load Balancer for the application tier and the Classic Load Balancer for the web tier
  C. Create a Classic Load Balancer and add multiple targets for the Web and Application tiers
  D. Create separate Classic Load Balancers for the Web and Application tiers

Answer: **A**

Explanation: You may upload or remove your load balancer as your requirements change, without disrupting the general glide of requests on your software. Elastic Load Balancing scales your load balancer as site visitors for your application changes, over the years. Elastic Load Balancing can scale to the enormous majority of workloads routinely.

76- A company sets up Classic Load Balancer with EC2 instances running behind them, and the instances are spun-up through an auto-scaling group. It is noticed that there is a spike in traffic at the start and end of the day. The ELB and auto-scaling groups were configured with the default settings. There are timeouts, and half rendered pages that occur at times. How would the company resolve this issue?

    A. By changing the maximum number of instances setting in the Auto-Scaling Group
    B. By changing the Connection Draining timeout in the ELB
    C. By enabling Cross Zone Load Balancing
    D. By adding another Auto-Scaling Group to the ELB

Answer: **B**

Explanation: When auto-scaling is terminating the instance, the requests are partially fulfilled or not completed. In this case, you can increase the connection draining on ELB.

77- A company needs to establish a VPN connection between AWS and its on-premises infrastructure. It has the following demands:
- Support for RSA 4096-bit encryption
- Radius/NT domain user authentication function
- Deep-inspect packet logging function

What can be done to achieve these requirements?
    A. Use an AWS managed VPN
    B. Use a VPN from the AWS market place
    C. Use AWS Direct Connect with a Private VIF
    D. Use AWS Direct Connect with a Public VIF

Answer: **B**

Explanation: The requirements are very specific, so you need to use VPN connection from the AWS market place.

78- A Load Balancer is created in AWS with EC2 instances behind them. The ELB is serving users on the internet. The web servers behind the ELB are stateful web servers, and users complain of intermittent issue while accessing the website. How can you resolve this issue?

    A. By ensuring that the Security group for the web servers are open on port 443

B. By ensuring that the Security group for the web servers are open for 0.0.0.0/0
C. Be enabling sticky sessions on the load balancer
D. By enabling connection draining

Answer: **C**

Explanation: The sticky session is the mechanism used to route requests to the same target within a target group. It is useful for the server that maintains the state information to provide continuous experience to the users.

79- A company has the following requirements:

- Transfer data from an on-premises Hadoop cluster to AWS
- Data transfer that can run up to 1Gbps to 1.5Gbps
- Consistent and fault tolerant data transfer on AWS

What can be used to achieve these requirements?
A. A single 1Gbps AWS Direct Connect connection with an AWS VPN backup
B. Two 1 Gbps AWS Direct Connect Connection with an AWS VPN backup
C. Three 1Gbps AWS Direct Connect Connection
D. Two 1Gbps AWS Direct Connect Connection with two AWS VPN backup

Answer: **C**

Explanation: Three AWS Direct Connect Connections are required. Two are used for normal data transfer while one is used for backup in case of failure in connection. Other options are incorrect because VPN does not provide consistent data transfer.

80- A company wants to use VPC via AWS Direct Connect Connection in the us-west region. The VPC is located in another region. How can this connectivity be performed? (Choose 2)

A. By creating a Private VIF from the current AWS Direct Connect Connection. This is possible with inter-region peering
B. By creating a Direct Connect gateway in a public region
C. By creating a public VIF and then a VPN connection over that to the remote VPC
D. By creating a private VIF and then a VPN connection over that to the remote VPC

Answer: **B & C**

Explanation: You can create Direct Connect gateway in any public region and use it to connect AWS Direct Connect connection over the private virtual interface to VPCs in your account that

is located in the different region. You can also create a virtual public interface for your AWS Direct Connect connection and then create a VPN connection to your VPC in the remote region.

81- A company has an EC2 instance that acts as a custom origin for CloudFront web distribution. The traffic must be encrypted completely in the transit. How can this be performed?

    A. By configuring the Viewer protocol policy as Redirect HTTP to HTTPS and changing the origin protocol policy to Match Viewer

    B. By configuring the Viewer protocol policy as HTTP and ensuring that SSL certificate is installed on the EC2 instance

    C. By configuring the Viewer protocol policy as HTTPs and ensuring that the traffic flows via the Amazon Virtual Private Network

    D. By configuring the Viewer protocol policy as Redirect HTTP to HTTPs and ensuring that the traffic flows via the Amazon Virtual Private Network

Answer: **A**

Explanation: If you require HTTPS to communicate between CloudFront and your custom origin, you must use the domain name that CloudFront assigned to your distribution in the URLs for your objects. Change the **Origin Protocol Policy** setting for the applicable origins in your distribution. Install an SSL/TLS certificate on your custom origin server (this is not required when you use an Amazon S3 origin).

82- For creating an AWS workspace, which of the following is required?

    A. A VPC with a private and public subnet

    B. A User directory

    C. A NAT instance on the customer side

    D. An AWS Direct Connect Connection

Answer: **B**

Explanation: When creating a workspace, you need to choose the Existing User Directory.

83- Your company has created an AWS Direct Connect Connection, and a virtual private gateway is attached to a VPC. Almost 111 routes are being advertised from the on-premises. A private

VIF is being created to VPGW but the Virtual Interface is showing down. What needs to be done to make sure that the interface comes up again?

   A. Ensure that a VPN connection is also in place for the tunnel to become active
   B. Ensure less routes are being advertised
   C. Ensure that static routes are put in place
   D. Ensure that the IPsec configuration is correct

Answer: **B**

Explanation: The main problem is that more than 100 routes are being advertised. Therefore, the tunnel is not coming up.

84-You created a VPC endpoint for your SaaS product that is hosted on AWS. You provided a link to the customers for accessing this from their applications, which work on UDP protocol. You also provided DNS name for the link. However, the customers are not capable of using the link from within their application. What could be the problem?

   A. The gateway endpoint has a policy that denies access. This should be modified accordingly
   B. The service endpoint only works on the TCP protocol
   C. The customer needs to create a Network Load Balancer to access the endpoint service
   D. The customer needs to use a NAT device to access the endpoint service

Answer: **B**

Explanation: You could create your application in your VPC and configure it as an AWS private-link-powered carrier (called an endpoint provider). Different AWS principals can create a connection from their VPC on your endpoint service using an interface VPC endpoint. You are the carrier issuer, and the AWS principals that create connections in your carrier are carrier customers.

85-A VPC has a set of instances. You have a requirement to host an application in the VPC which communicates on IPv6. How can you fulfil this requirement? (Choose 2).

   A. By disabling IPv4 for the subnet
   B. By disabling IPv4 for the VPC
   C. By enabling IPv6 for the subnet
   D. By enabling IPv6 for the VPC

Answer: C & D

Explanation: You can enable IPV6 support on your VPC and resources. Your VPC cannot operate in dual-stack mode. Your resource can communicate over IPV4, IPV6 and both but their communications are independent of each other.

86- You have set up an EC2 instance in VPC. You are trying to ping the instance but are not able to do so. You have verified the following:

- Internet gateway attached to the VPC
- Route tables added for the internet gateway
- IP address assigned to the internet

You have enabled the VPC flow logs and can watch the rejection requests for the outgoing traffic

- 2123456789111eni-3456b8ca 54.0.113.12 172.31.16.140 0 0 1 4 336 1432917142 ACCEPT OK
- 2123456789111eni-3456b8ca 172.31.16.140 54.0.113.12 0 0 1 4 336 1432917142 REJECT OK

What can be done to make sure that ping request works?
A. Ensure that the NACL allows inbound ICMP requests
B. Ensure that the NACL allows outbound ICMP requests
C. Ensure that the Security Group allows inbound ICMP requests
D. Ensure that the Security Group allows outbound ICMP requests

Answer: B

Explanation: Since the outgoing traffic is blocked, that means NACl does not allow the outbound traffic to flow.

87- A company sets up a set of EC2 instances behind a Load Balancer, and there seems to be the barrage of requests from series of URLs. Now, you need to blacklist these URLs. How can you do this in an ongoing manner?

A. By denying the URLs via the Security Groups for instance
B. By denying the URLs via the NACLs for the subnet
C. By putting a WAF in front of the Application Load Balancer
D. By using AWS VPC flow logs to prevent the attacks from the URLs

Answer: C

Explanation: WAF is a Web Application Firewall that helps you to protect your web application from common web exploits that can affect your application availability, compromise on security, and consume excessive resources.

88-To set up a Cross Connect with AWS Direct Connect, you already have the necessary equipment. Now, you need to complete the connection process. How would you do it?

    A. By contacting your provider

    B. By raising a support ticket with AWS

    C. By raising an AWS Direct Connect request in the AWS console

    D. By contacting an AWS partner

Answer: A

Explanation: After downloading the Letter of Authorization and Connecting Facility Assignment (LOA-CFA), you need to complete the cross-connection also known as Cross Connect. If you have the equipment in AWS Direct Connect location, contact the appropriate provider for the connection's establishment. After the Cross Connect is configured, you can create the virtual interfaces by using AWS Direct Connect Console.

89-You need to manage a threat detection service that continuously monitors the malicious and unauthorized behavior against the EC2 instances. Which application can help for this requirement?

    A. Amazon GuardDuty

    B. Amazon CloudTrail

    C. Amazon VPC Flow Logs

    D. Amazon CloudWatch Logs

Answer: A

Explanation: Amazon Guard Duty is a managed service that continuously monitors the threat from malicious and unauthorized resources to protect your AWS accounts and workloads.

90-Your company sets up a series of EC2 instances in VPC. Now, there is a need to set up management work within the VPC. Which of the following is the part of the implementation step?

    A. Attaching multiple Elastic Network Interfaces to an instance
    B. Attaching multiple public IP addresses to an existing Elastic Network Interface for instance
    C. Attaching multiple elastic IP addresses to an existing Elastic Network Interface for instance
    D. Attaching multiple private IP addresses to an existing Elastic Network Interface for instance

Answer: **A**

Explanation: You can create a network interface, attach it to an instance, detach it from an instance, and attach it to another instance. A network interface's attributes follow it as it is attached or detached from an instance and re-attached to another instance. When you move a network interface from one instance to another, network traffic is redirected to the new instance.

91- A company wants to connect their on-premises location with AWS VPC. The on-premises server is capable of resolving custom DNS server domain name in the VPC, and the instances in the VPC needs to have the ability to resolve the DNS names of the on-premises server. What steps should be taken to do this?

    A. Setup a DNS forwarder in your VPC. Ensure the DNS forwarder points to the Amazon DNS resolver for the VPC. Ensure the forwarder is configured with the on-premises DNS server. Change the option set for the VPC for the IP address of the DNS forwarder. Configure a DNS forwarder in the on-premises location
    B. Setup a DNS forwarder in your VPC. Ensure the DNS forwarder points to the name server for the Route53 hosted zone. Ensure the forwarder is configured with the on-premises DNS server. Change the option set for the VPC for the IP address of the DNS forwarder. Configure a DNS forwarder in the on-premises location
    C. Setup a DNS forwarder in your VPC. Ensure the DNS forwarder points to the IP address of the on-premises DNS server. Change the option set for the VPC for the IP address of the DNS forwarder. Configure a DNS forwarder in the on-premises location
    D. Setup a DNS forwarder in your VPC. Ensure the DNS forwarder points to the IP address of the VPN tunnel. Change the option set for the VPC for the IP address of the DNS forwarder. Configure a DNS forwarder in the on-premises location

Answer: A

Explanation: Unbound allows resolution of requests originating from AWS by forwarding them to your on-premises environment—and vice versa. For this, just focus on a basic installation of Amazon Linux with the configuration necessary to direct traffic to on-premises environments or the Amazon VPC–provided DNS, as appropriate.

92- You are creating a VPN connection between your on-premises infrastructure and AWS. You have established a Virtual Private Gateway and a Customer Gateway. You have to make sure that the firewall rules are set on your side. Which of the following shoud you consider? (Choose 2)

    A. TCP Port 500
    B. TCP Port 50
    C. UDP Port 500
    D. UDP Port 50
    E. IP Protocol 5
    F. IP Protocol 50

Answer: C & F

Explanation: To use this service, you must have an internet-routable IP address to use as the endpoint for the IPSec tunnels connecting your customer gateway to the Virtual Private Gateway. If a firewall is in place between the internet and your gateway, the rules in the following tables must be in place to establish the IPsec tunnels. The Virtual Private Gateway addresses are in the configuration information that you get from the integration team.

93- About Amazon CloudFront Cache behavior, which of the following statement is false?

    A. For RTMP distributions, you can configure CloudFront to forward query string parameters to your origin
    B. You can forward query strings to the origin and cache based on all parameters in the query string
    C. You can forward query strings to the origin and cache based on specified parameters in the query string
    D. You cannot forward query strings to the origin and CloudFront does not cache based on query string parameters

Answer: A

Explanation: For RTMP distribution, you cannot configure the CloudFront to forward the query string parameters to your origin.

94- You have to see all the port scans that are occurring on a couple of EC2 instances. Which of the following can be used to achieve this requirement?

    A. AWS Inspector
    B. AWS Trusted Advisor
    C. AWS VPC Flow Logs
    D. AWS CloudWatch Events

Answer: **C**

Explanation: AWS VPC Flow Logs is the feature that enables you to capture the information about the IP traffic going to and from the network interface in your VPC. Flow Log data is stored using the Amazon CloudWatch logs.

95- You are creating a fault-tolerant EC2 instance by creating a secondary network interface and a backup EC2 instance. Which of the following is used to ensure the switch over? (Choose 2)

    A. The network interface must reside in the same availability zone
    B. The network interface must reside in a different availability zone
    C. The instance must reside in the same availability zone
    D. The instance must reside in different availability zone

Answer: **A & C**

Explanation: You can attach a network interface in one subnet in an instance to another subnet inside the same VPC. Both the network interface and the instance must reside in the same availability zone.

96- A company sets up a host of networking component in AWS. They have put out stringent control in place to make sure that networking components are charged by IT personnel. Additionally, they must get notified for any unwanted access to networking components. Which of the following options is used in this case?

    A. AWS VPC Flow Logs
    B. AWS CloudTrail

    C. AWS Trusted Advisor

    D. AWS Inspector

Answer: **B**

Explanation: AWS CloudTrail provides the history of API calls for an account, including the API calls made through the management console, SDK's, command line tools and higher-level AWS services.

97- You have established a VPN connection between your on-premises and AWS VPC. You have to make sure that the instances in the VPC can reach the internet, so you also have to attach an internet gateway. What can you to maintain the route table and ensure that the traffic flows via VPN and the internet?

    A. Setup 2 route tables. One route table with the default route to the internet and another one with the default route to the Virtual Private Gateway. Attach the route tables to the subnets in the VPC

    B. Setup one route table. Add one route of 0.0.0.0/0 to the internet and one specific prefix route for the Virtual Private Gateway. Attach the route table to the subnets in the VPC

    C. Setup one route table. Add one route of 0.0.0.0/0 to the internet and another route of 0.0.0.0/0 route for the Virtual Private Gateway. Attach the route table to the subnets in the VPC

    D. Setup 2 route tables. One route table with the default route to the internet and another one with the specific prefix route to the Virtual Private Gateway. Attach the route tables to the subnets in the VPC

Answer: **B**

Explanation: AWS Managed VPN Connections are used to enable instances in your VPC to communicate with your network. To perform this, create and attach a Virtual Private Gateway to your VPC and then add the route with a destination of your network and a target of the Virtual Private Gateway. You can then create and configure your VPN connection.

98- A MySQL cluster is hosted in AWS, and the nodes within cluster work with private IP addresses. A self-referencing security group is present that is used for securing access across the nodes of the cluster. Now, there is a requirement to ensure disaster recovery for these nodes in another region. How can you achieve the communication across the different regions between the nodes?

A. By using public IP addresses and SSL certificates for secure communication across the nodes

B. By using the private IP addresses of the nodes and SSL certificates for secure communication across those nodes

C. By creating a VPN IPSec tunnel and ensuring that the nodes in different regions refer to the security groups assigned to the nodes in the primary region

D. By creating a VPN IPSec tunnel and ensuring that the nodes in different regions refer to the VPC CIDR block in their security groups

Answer: **D**

Explanation: You need to use the IPSec VPN tunnel to provide secure communication across the internet between the regions.

99- A CloudFormation template is designed to provide the infrastructure of your company's account. Resources can be created primarily. Besides CloudFormation, the company wants to get notified through automated alarms if any resource is created. What can be used for this? (Choose 3)

A. AWS Config

B. AWS Lambda

C. Simple Notification Service

D. CloudFormation

E. Ops Work

F. CloudWatch logs

Answer: **A, B, & C**

Explanation: AWS Config is specially used for this purpose. Any resource update can trigger a Lambda function and notification via the SNS service.

100- An application is set up on an EC2 instance in a private subnet. The instances are used to process videos and are enabled with Enhanced Networking. Now, the instances require videos from S3 bucket for processing. An IAM role has been assigned to the instances to access the S3 but when instances try to access the S3, an error 403 is shown. How can you resolve this error?

A. By ensuring that VPC endpoint is created and associated with subnets via route tables that are created inside selected VPC

B. By ensuring that a VPC endpoint is created and attached to the EC2 instance

C. By ensuring that the CIDR range for the S3 bucket is added to the security groups for the EC2 instance

D. By ensuring that the CIDR range for the S3 bucket is added to the NACLs for the subnet

Answer: A

Explanation: You need to set up a gateway endpoint for this as the VPC endpoints need to be associated with the EC2 instance.

101-   A company has created a VPC endpoint for the private subnet to access S3. The default endpoint policy is in place, and you are trying to access the bucket, but the access is denied. What needs to be done?

A. Add the VPC endpoint to endpoint policy for allowing access to the S3 bucket

B. Add the VPC to the S3 bucket policy

C. Add the VPC endpoint to the S3 bucket policy

D. Add the VPC endpoint to the bucket ACL

Answer: C

Explanation: You need to make sure that the S3 bucket policy allows access to the VPC endpoints.

102-   You plan to set up an AWS VPN Managed Connection. You have a Customer gateway behind a NAT device. What steps should be taken to ensure proper connectivity in this case? (Choose 2)

A. Use the public IP address of the NAT device

B. Use the private IP address of the customer gateway

C. Ensure that the on-premises firewall has UDP port 4500 unblocked

D. Ensure that the on-premises firewall has TCP port 4500 unblocked

Answer: A & C

Explanation: The public IP address must be static. In case the customer gateway is behind the NAT device that is enabled for NAT traversal, use the public IP address of NAT device and adjust the rules of the firewall to unblock UDP port 4500.

103-   A set of EC2 instances is created in VPC. You need to ensure that the logs created from the specific location on the EC2 instances are sent to a central log location. How can you achieve this? (Choose 2)

    A. By using the Cloud Watch Logs agent
    B. By using the AWS Inspector agent
    C. By centralizing the logs to a Cloud Watch Logs Group
    D. By centralizing the Logs to a VPC Log group

Answer: **A & C**

Explanation: To collect logs from your Amazon EC2 instances and on-premises servers into CloudWatch Logs, AWS gives both a brand new unified CloudWatch agent and an older CloudWatch Logs agent. We recommend the unified CloudWatch agent, which has the following benefits:

- You may collect both logs and advanced metrics with the set up and configuration of just one agent
- The unified agent enables the collection of logs from servers logging windows Server
- If you are using the agent to collect CloudWatch metrics, the unified agent additionally permits the collection of extra device metrics, for in-guest visibility

104-   A company has the following setup in AWS:
- Set of EC2 instances that are hosting a web application
- An application load balancer placed in front of EC2 instances

Some malicious requests are coming from the set of IP addresses. Which one of the following is used to protect against these requests?

    A. Security Groups
    B. VPC Flow Logs
    C. AWS Inspector
    D. AWS WAF

Answer: **D**

Explanation: AWS WAF can be used to protect Application Load Balancer and CloudFront.

105- You have set up an EC2 instance that hosts a web application. You have the following set of rules:

Security Group Rules:

- Allow inbound traffic at port 80 from 0.0.0.0/0 and deny the outgoing traffic
- NACL
- Allow inbound traffic at port 80 from 0.0.0.0/0 and deny the outbound traffic

Now, the users are complaining that they cannot access the web server. What can be done to resolve this issue?
   A. Allow outgoing traffic on the security groups for port 80
   B. Allow outgoing traffic on the NACL for port 80
   C. Allow outgoing traffic on the security groups for ephemeral ports
   D. Allow outgoing traffic on the NACL for ephemeral ports

Answer: **D**

Explanation: The client that initiates the request chooses the ephemeral port range. The range varies depending on the customer's operating gadget. Many Linux kernels (which include the Amazon Linux kernel) use ports 32768-61000. Requests originating from Elastic Load Balancing use ports 1024-65535. Windows OS structures through Windows Server 2003 use ports 1025-5000. Windows Server 2008 and later variations use ports 49152-65535. A NAT gateway uses ports 1024-65535.

106- You need to automate the VPC peering connections that occur in your AWS account. Which of the following method can be used?

   A. Use a CloudFormation template to peer the VPCs
   B. Use an OpsWorks Stack to peer the VPCs
   C. Use CloudTrail along with a Lambda function
   D. Use CloudWatch metrics along with a Lambda function

Answer: **A**

Explanation: VPC Peering connection enables a network connection between two VPCs, so that you can route traffic between them by using a private IP address.

107- A company plans to deliver content via an application hosted on a set of EC2 instances. The end devices can be anything like laptop, mobile, tablets, etc. The content needs to be

optimized based on the end user device. Which of the following can help in this with minimum cost and easier deployment strategy? (Choose 2)

    A. Application Load Balancers
    B. CloudFront with Lambda Edge
    C. Network Load Balancers
    D. Appstream 2.0

Answer: **A & B**

Explanation: Application Load Balancer is used to distribute the processing powers to different instances based on the type of request. CloudFront can return different objects to the viewer based on the device they are using by checking the User-agent header, which includes the information about the device.

108-   You are planning to set up a VPC with subnets. The EC2 instances hosted in the VPC need to get the time from custom NTP server. How can you perform this?

    A. By creating a DHCP options set and providing the NTP server name
    B. By defining a resource record in Route 53 and providing the NTP server name
    C. By assigning the NTP server in the subnet configuration
    D. By using an Application Load Balancer and then providing the NTP server as part of the ELB configuration

Answer: **A**

Explanation: You can create a new DCP option set and then provide the NTP server name as part of the options set.

109-   A company requires CPN connectivity to an AWS VPC. There are almost 100 mobile devices, 40 remote computers, and a site office that needs to be connected. How can you achieve this connectivity? (Choose 2)

    A. By using AWS Managed VPN for the site office
    B. By using AWS Managed VPN for the mobile and remoting computers
    C. By using a custom VPN server to accept connections from the mobile and remote computers
    D. By using AWS Direct Connect with a public VIF for the site office

Answer: **A & C**

Explanation: For the site office, Standard AWS Managed VPN is used. You need to use a custom VPN server since there is no mechanism currently for point-to-site connectivity for individual devices.

110-   A company sets up an AWS Direct Connect Connection for their on-premises location. An application in the on-premises location wants to access the DynamoDB table. All the data written in DynamoDB is encrypted. How can you enable such a requirement?

    A. By setting up a Private VIF

    B. By setting up a Public VIF

    C. By setting up an IPSec VPN over a private VIF

    D. By setting up an IPSec VPN over a public VIF

Answer: **D**

Explanation: You can use AWS Direct Connect to establish a dedicated network connection between your network. Create a logical connection to public AWS resources, such as an Amazon Virtual Private Gateway IPsec endpoint. This solution combines the AWS managed benefits of the VPN solution with low latency, increased bandwidth, more consistent benefits of the AWS Direct Connect solution, and an end-to-end, secure IPSec connection.

111- A Cloud Front distribution is set up on AWS, and you are going to conduct a primary test to check the performance of the Cloud Front distribution. Which factors must be kept in mind while performing the load test? (Choose 2)

    A. Ensure to initiate client's requests from multiple geographic regions

    B. Configure your test, so each client makes an independent DNS request

    C. Ensure that client requests hit the origin server

    D. Ensure that SSL is turned on for the distribution

Answer: **A & B**

Explanation: CloudFront is designed to scale for the viewers who have different client IP addresses and different DNS resolver across multiple geographic regions.

112-A company has AWS DirectConnect in the us-west region. They are currently using public VIF to access the S3 bucket in the us-west region. Now, they want to make the use of AWS

Direct Connect to access the S3 bucket in the us-east region. How can this be done most economically?

   A. By creating another AWS Direct Connect Connection from your on-premises network in the us-east region
   B. By creating another private VIF from your current AWS Direct Connect Connection
   C. By creating another public VIF from your current AWS Direct Connect Connection
   D. By creating a VPN IPSec connection

Answer: **C**

Explanation: AWS Direct Connect locations can access public services in any public region, or AWS Govt. Cloud can access public services in any other region.

113-A set of EC2 instances within the VPC is located in us-east-1. You require optimal networking performance in these instances. These instances will communicate to other instances in VPCs located in us-east-2 through VPC peering. Which of the following options is applicable to ensure the maximum network performance? (Choose 2)

   A. Enabling Enhanced Networking on the instances
   B. Setting the MTU on the instances to 9001
   C. Ensuring the operating system supports Enhanced Networking
   D. Creating two availability zones for the instances in the primary VPC and placing them in a placement group

Answer: **A & C**

Explanation: Enhanced Networking uses the single root I/O virtualization to provide the high-performance capabilities to network on supported instance types. Enhanced Networking provides higher bandwidth, higher packets per second performance and lower inter-instance latencies.

114-   A Classic Load Balancer is set up and EC2 instances are behind the Load Balancer. The following Security Groups have been set:

Security Group for the ELB: Accept the incoming traffic coming on port 80 from 0.0.0.0/0
Security Group for the EC2 instances: Accept the incoming traffic coming on port 80 from 0.0.0.0/0.

You notice that EC2 instances are getting a large number of direct requests from the internet. How can you resolve this issue?

    A. By changing the ELB security group to only accept traffic from the EC2 instances on port 80

    B. By changing the EC2 instance security group to only accept traffic from the ELB security group on port 80

    C. By changing the ELB security group to only accept traffic from the EC2 instances on port 443

    D. By changing the EC2 instance security group to only accept traffic from the ELB security group on port 443

Answer: **B**

Explanation: The security groups for your instances must allow them to communicate with the load balancer.

115-A company has multiple VPCs, one for development, one for staging, one for production, and one for management. It is required that the traffic should flow from other VPCs to the management VPC. The VPCs should be traversable through the on-premises infrastructure. How can you develop the solution with minimum efforts?

    A. By creating a VPC peering connection between the VPCs and a VPN connection between the management VPC and the on-premises environment

    B. By creating a VPC peering connection between the VPCs and a VPN connection between all the VPCs and the on-premises environment

    C. By creating a Virtual Private Gateway connection between all of the VPCs and a VPN connection between the management VPC and the on-premises environment

    D. By creating a VPN connection between the management VPC and all the other VPCs. Also, by creating a VPN connection between management VPC and the on-premises environment

Answer: **B**

Explanation: Create a shared services VPC that includes replicate services, and also application proxies for requests to a remote resource that cannot be replicated as a shared service. This removes the need to create VPN connections for added VPCs because all required on-premises assets can be accessed either at once or they cannot be accessed directly through the shared service VPC.

116- A hosted zone is configured in Route 53. You are required to check the types of records being requested to the zone. How can you implement this?

    A. By configuring VPC Flow logs
    B. By configuring Amazon Route 53 logging
    C. By configuring CloudWatch metrics
    D. By configuring CloudTrail

Answer: **B**

Explanation: You can configure the Amazon Route 53 to log information about the queries that Route 53 receives, which are; domain and subdomain that is requested, the date and the time of the request, the DNS record, the Route 53 edge location that responded to the query generated by DNS, and the DNS response code.

117-An application hosted on AWS uses Cloud HSM to get SSL certificates. These certificates are installed on EC2 instances behind an Auto Scaling Group. How can the scaling of Cloud HSM modules be ensured with EC2 instances to make the on-time delivery of SSL certificates?

    A. By creating a Network Load Balancer and placing the Cloud HSM device behind it
    B. By just specifying the number of HSM modules in the cluster
    C. By creating an Application Load Balancer and placing the Cloud HSM device behind it
    D. By creating another Auto Scaling Group for the Cloud HSM modules

Answer: **B**

Explanation: AWS Cloud HSM provides the hardware security modules in the cluster. A cluster is the collection of the individual HSMs that keeps in sync by AWS Cloud HSM. You can place it in multiple availability zones and in multiple regions. Spreading the cluster across multiple regions and availability zones increases the redundancy and availability.

118- A company plans to use AWS EC2 and ELB for the web application deployment but the security policy informs that all the traffic must be encrypted. Which of the following options ensure that these requirements will be established? (Choose 2)

    A. Ensure the load balancer listens on port 80
    B. Ensure the load balancer listens on port 443

C. Ensure the HTTPS listener sends requests to the instances on port 443

D. Ensure the HTTPS listener sends requests to the instances on port 80

Answer: **B & C**

Explanation: You can establish a load balancer that listens on both the port HTTP 80 and HTTP 443. The HTTPS listener sends the requests to the instances on port 443 and the communication between the load balancer. The instances are encrypted.

119-   To perform a deep packet analysis on the packets that are sent to your EC2 instance, which one the following services will help you?

A. Wireshark

B. AWS CloudTrail

C. AWS CloudWatch

D. AWS VPC Flow Logs

Answer: **A**

Explanation: If you want to use a packet analysis tool, external tools must be implemented for this purpose. Wireshark performs detailed packet analysis and tracing.

120-   You want to create a Private VIF for AWS Direct Connect connection. Which of the following is required during the configuration? (Choose 2)

A. The Peer Public IP

B. VLAN ID

C. Virtual Gateway

D. Prefixes to advertise

Answer: **B & C**

Explanation: A Public Virtual Interface can be created to connect to the public resources or can create a Private Virtual Interface to connect to your VPC.

121-You have created an Application Load Balancer, and you want to point your domain names of www.example.com and example.com to the application load balancer. Your hosted zone is example.com. How can you perform this?

A. By creating one CNAME record for the ELB to www.example.com, and then creating another CNAME record to the ELB to example.com

B. By creating an ALIAS record for example.com and pointing it to the ELB as the target. You must also create a CNAME record for www.example.com and point it to example.com

C. By creating an ALIAS record for the ELB and pointing it to example.com. you must also create a PTR record for www.example.com and point it to example.com

D. By creating one CNAME record for the ELB to www.example.com, and then creating another PTR record to the ELB to example.com

Answer: **B**

Explanation: Amazon Route 53 alias record provides the Route 53 specific extension to DNS functionality. Alias records let you route your traffic to selected AWS resources such as CloudFront distribution and S3 bucket.

122- A private hosted zone is set up in Route 53. You have set up a VPN connection between the AWS VPC and on-premises network. You need to make sure that you can resolve the DNS names from the on-premises to the resource records that are defined in the private hosted zone. What steps should be taken to perform this?

A. Create a DNS resolver server in your on-premises location. Configure the VPC with a new DHCP option set that uses this DNS resolver

B. Create a DNS forwarder server in your on-premises location. Configure the VPC with a new DHCP option set that uses this DNS forwarder

C. Configure a DNS forwarder in the VPC that will forward DNS requests to the Route 53 private hosted zone

D. Configure a DNS resolver in the VPC that will forward DNS requests to the Route 53 private hosted zone

Answer: **C**

Explanation: You can resolve your domain name in a private hosted zone from your on-premises network by configuring the DNS resolver.

123- A company needs to create VPN based EC2 instances. These instances should allow the communication between two VPCs in different regions. You have established one instance in

one VPC subnet while the other instance in another VPC subnet and the connection is established via the internet gateway. What will your next step be?

   A. Placing a NAT instance in front of both of the VPN connections
   B. Placing a Virtual Private Gateway as the termination endpoint
   C. Using a private hosted zone in Route 53
   D. Having multiple VPN instances for high availability

Answer: **D**

Explanation: High availability of the instances must be considered. In AWS Managed VPN, there are 2 tunnels created, providing the high availability in place. If the instance goes down, the connection will be broken.

124-   You have some instances present in the private subnet in VPC. You have provisioned a NAT gateway in a public subnet to allow the instances in the private subnet to communicate with the internet. You are trying to ping the Elastic IP of the NAT gateway from the workstation but are unable to do so. How can you resolve this issue?

   A. By changing the security groups assigned to the NAT gateway to allow incoming ICMP traffic
   B. By changing the NACL's assigned to the public subnet hosting the NAT gateway to allow incoming and outgoing ICMP traffic
   C. By pinging the public IP address of the NAT gateway instead of the Elastic IP
   D. This is not possible, since this is how the NAT gateway works

Answer: **D**

Explanation: If you are trying to ping the Elastic IP address of the NAT or private IP address from the internet or any of the instances within VPC, you will not get a response because the NAT gateway does not respond to the ping command.

125-   VPC and EC2 instances are hosted in the subnet. You need to diagnose the layer seven traffic and check which requests are ACCEPTED and REJECTED. Which of the following would help in fulfilling these requirements?

   A. Enabling CloudTrail
   B. Installing IDS on each instance
   C. Installing VPC Flow Logs

D. Using CloudWatch Logs

Answer: **C**

Explanation: VPC Flow Logs are used to fulfill this requirement. It is the feature that enables you to capture the ingoing and outgoing traffic in network interface within the VPC.

126- A Linux instance has a connectivity issue, and you are trying to diagnose it. The instance is linked to the public IP and public subnet. The internet gateway is attached, and the routing table is on the place. You SSH into the instance from a bastion host. You performed the ifconfig command and found out that the interface does not have a public IP address. How can you check this issue?

    A. By assigning the public IP to the interface
    B. By assigning an Elastic IP to the interface
    C. By checking the security groups for the instance
    D. By assigning a private IP to the interface

Answer: **C**

Explanation: You can check the security groups to see that the instance is accepting traffic from the internet or not.

127- A company plans to set up an AWS Direct Connect connection along with the private VIF. The company has 169 private prefixes that will be advertised through the private VIF. The company has raised the request and made sure that the equipment is in place. What is the best implementation step for the desired connection?

    A. Ensuring to create a public VIF to access the resources in the VPC
    B. Summarizing the routes into a default route
    C. Creating a VPN Connection
    D. Ensuring a VPC peering connection is in place

Answer: **B**

Explanation: While troubleshooting the AWS Direct Connect, the main issue is that the number of IP prefixes summarized is below 100. Therefore, one of the main steps is to ensure that the routes are being summarized into the default route.

128- You are creating a CloudFormation template that will be used for provisioning of VPCs and subnets. You need to allow the dynamic provisioning aspect as to which AZ, the subnets need to be created. Which part of the template will help in dynamic provisioning values?

    A. Parameters
    B. Outputs
    C. Tags
    D. Change Sets

Answer: **A**

Explanation: Use the optional parameters to customize the template. Parameters enable you to input the custom values to your template each time you update or create a stack.

129- A VPC peering connection is set up between two VPCs, VPC A and VPC B. You are trying to ping the VPC in each instance to the other but are unable to do so. You have verified the security groups for the instances and NACLs, and confirmed that the ICMP traffic is allowed. How can you resolve this issue? (Choose 2)

    A. By adding a route in the route table in VPC A to VPC B via the VPC peering connection
    B. By adding a route in the route table in VPC A to VPC B via the internet gateway
    C. By adding a route in the route table in VPC B to VPC A via the VPC peering connection
    D. By adding a route in the route table in VPC B to VPC A via the internet gateway

Answer: **A & C**

Explanation: A VPC peering connection is the connection between two VPCs that allows them to communicate or route the traffic using IPV4 addresses. Instances in VPC can communicate to each other as they are a part of the same network.

130- You are trying to implement the following architecture:

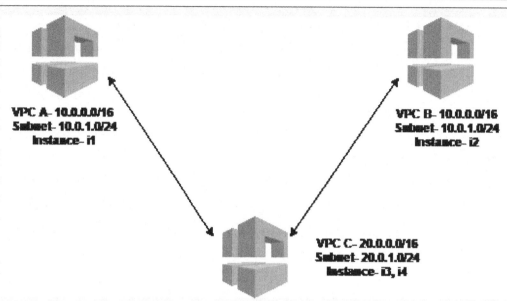

So, you have a VPC peering connection between VPC A and VPC C and the second one between VPC B and VPC C and you have instances defined in each subnet. Now you need to ensure the following:

- Instance i3 can communicate to instance i1 but cannot with instance i2
- Instance i4 can communicate with instance i2 but cannot with i1

What could be the methods to accomplish this? (Choose 2)

    A. Create two subnets in VPC C, ensure i3 and i4 are in different subnets

    B. Ensure different route tables are created to restrict access and added to the two different subnets

    C. Ensure that i3 and i4 are created in the same subnet

    D. Ensure that one route table is created which restricts access and added to the subnet

Answer: **A & B**

Explanation: Both VPC A and VPC B have overlapping CIDRs. Therefore, it is difficult to restrict the traffic if you only have one subnet. Hence, create two different subnets with two different route tables to meet the requirement.

131-As per the TCP/IP model, which layer makes use of the core protocols of Transmission Control Protocol (TCP) and the User Datagram Protocol (UDP)

    A. Transport Layer

    B. Session Layer

    C. Datalink Layer

    D. Network Layer

Answer: A

Explanation: The transport layer (also referred to as the host-to-host transport layer) offers session and datagram communication services to the application layer. The Transmission Control Protocol (TCP) and the User Datagram Protocol (UDP) are the core protocols for the Transport layer.

132- Choose the option that can help you to create dual homed on different subnet using workloads/roles.

    A. Multiple VPCs
    B. Multiple Network Interfaces
    C. Multiple S3 Bucket
    D. Multiple EBS Volumes

Answer: B

Explanation: Attaching multiple network interface to an instance allows you to create a low budget and high availability solution, management network, dual-homed instances with workloads/roles on distinct subnets and is useful for network and security appliances in your VPC.

133- A user developed a CIDR 20.0.0.0/24. He created a CIDR 20.0.0.0/25 public subnet and a CIDR 20.0.0.128/25 private subnet and launched a single instance in both private and public subnet. Which of the given options is not possible with the right IP address (private IP assigned to a public or private subnet instance)?

    A. 20.0.0.122
    B. 20.0.0.255
    C. 20.0.0.55
    D. 20.0.0.132

Answer: B

Explanation: Option B is correct because AWS reserves this IP address. You are not provided with nor can you assign the initial four IP addresses and the last IP address for each CIDR block subnet. For example, the following five IP addresses are reserved for a subnet with CIDR block 10.0.0.0/24:

- 10.0.0.0: Network Address

- 10.0.0.1: Reserved by AWS for the VPC router
- 10.0.0.2: Reserved by AWS. The IP address of the DNS server is always the base of the VPC network range plus two; however, we also reserve the base of each subnet range plus two. 10.0.0.3: Reserved by AWS for future use
- 10.0.0.255: Network Broadcast Address. We do not support broadcast in a VPC. Therefore, we reserve this address

134-   A user created a VPC subnet, launched an EC2 instance, and tried to access it via the Internet. During the initiation of the instance, the user has not chosen the option to assign the IP address. In this scenario, which of the given statement is true?

   A. The user can directly attach an elastic IP to the instance
   B. The instance will never launch if the public IP is not assigned
   C. The user would need to create an internet gateway and then attach an elastic IP to the instance to connect from internet
   D. The instance will always have a public DNS attached to the instance by default

Answer: **C**

Explanation: There is no internet gateway attached to the VPC when you create a simple subnet and VPC. To access it via the internet, you need to ensure that you have an internet gateway on the VPC and that the EC2 instance is allotted an Elastic or public IP to connect from internet.

135-   A set of t2.medium EC2 Instances have currently been deployed. It is now necessary to indicate that, between these instances low latency and high output are established. How can you do this while reducing downtime? (Choose 3)

   A. By launching new t2.medium instances from the AMIs
   B. By launching new m4.large instances from the AMIs
   C. By stopping and restarting the instances in a placement group
   D. By creating AMIs from the instances
   E. By ensuring that the new instances are launched in a placement group

Answer: **B, D, & E**
Explanation: A logical grouping of instances within a single Availability Zone is known as Placement group. They are recommended for applications that benefit from low network latency, high network throughput, or both.

Create AMIs from the instances to ensure minimum downtime so that new instances can be launched faster.

There is a limit to which instance types in a placement group may be used for EC2 instances. You cannot use T2.medium instances in a Placement group. So, use m4.large instances.

136-   A supplier must have access to an S3 bucket on your account. The supplier already has an AWS account. How can you give this bucket's access to the supplier?

    A. By creating a new IAM group and granting the relevant access to the vendor for that bucket

    B. By creating an S3 bucket policy that allows the vendor to read from the bucket from their AWS account

    C. By creating a new IAM user and grant the relevant access to the vendor on that bucket

    D. By creating a cross-account role for the vendor account and granting that role access to the S3 bucket

Answer: **D**

Explanation: You can share the resources with users in one account from another account. You do not have to create individual IAM users on every account if you have set cross-account access. Moreover, users do not have to sign out from one account in order to sign in to another account and access resources on different AWS accounts. You have an option to assign roles in your account that allow supplier to access S3 bucket in your account. After configuring the role, you can use the role from the AWS Management Console, the AWS CLI, and the API.

137-   Which of the following addresses would you use in order to send a broadcast message to your 10.0.0.0/24 subnet?

    A. 10.0.0.1

    B. 10.0.0.127

    C. 10.0.0.255

    D. The broadcast is not allowed in AWS

Answer: **D**

Explanation: AWS VPCs do not support broadcast or multicast.

138- A user creates a VPC subnet and launches an EC2 instance with default settings only. Which of the below mentioned options is ready to use on the EC2 instance as soon as it is launched?

    A. Internet Gateway
    B. Public IP
    C. Private IP
    D. Elastic IP

Answer: **C**

Explanation: Only the private IP is populated for EC2 instances when creating a subnet with the default settings. This cannot be done with the public IP, because by default, the public IP auto - assign will be 'no'. The Elastic IP and Internet gateway must also be configured manually.

139- An application is hosted on an EC2 instance. You plan to use the Content Delivery service to distribute content. There is a requirement to carry out a load test before going to production. In carrying out a load test involving the CDN service, which of these options must be considered? (Choose 3)

    A. Configure your test, so each client makes an independent DNS request
    B. Ensure that the request goes to the first IP returned by the DNS
    C. Send client requests from multiple geographic regions
    D. Spread your client requests across the set of IP addresses that are returned by DNS

Answer: **A, C, & D**

Explanation: The following points should be considered for load testing:

- Send client requests from multiple geographic regions
- Configure your test so that each client makes a separate DNS request; each client will then be given another set of DNS IP address
- Spread client requests through a set of IP addresses returned by DNS to each client that requests, which ensures that loads can be distributed on multiple servers at the edge location of CloudFront

140- An elastic IP address was associated with an instance for a 3-month period. Now the Elastic IP address has been disassociated. However, the Elastic IP address is still charged. What should you do so that the Elastic IP address stops being charged? (Choose 2)

A. Quickly associate it with any stopped instance
B. Quickly associate it with any running instance
C. Explicitly release the Elastic IP from your account
D. Associate it with an un-attached network interface

Answer: **B & C**

Explanation: In an event where a running Elastic IP address is not associated with an instance, or is associated with a stopped instance or an unconnected network port, AWS charges only a small hourly fee for efficiency with Elastic IP addresses. You do not get charged for a single Elastic IP address that is associated with the running instance, but you are charged for additional Elastic IP addresses associated with the instance. You can also explicitly release Elastic IP from your account.

141- When creating a hosted zone in Route 53, which of the following records are automatically created? (Choose 2)

A. AAA
B. CNAME
C. Name Server
D. SOA

Answer: **C & D**

Explanation: Amazon Route 53 automatically creates four Name Server (NS) records and a Start of Authority (SOA) record for the zone when creating your host zone.

142- VPCs located in different regions are required to be connected to each other. Which option cannot be used for connectivity?

A. VPC Peering
B. Internet-based VPN
C. Software to Hardware VPN
D. Software VPN

Answer: **A**

Explanation: Until November 2017, AWS did not support Cross-region VPC peering but for now, this is no longer the case. Therefore, by using VPC peering, you can connect to the VPCs located in different region.

143-   You have to create a VPC with the configuration "172.168.128.128/28". How many subnets can be created by using this configuration?

    A. 1
    B. 2
    C. 3
    D. 4

Answer: **A**

Explanation: The smallest permissible VPC CIDR range is /28 and maximum VPC CIDR range is /16, which means that no additional subnetting can take place for /28. Only one Subnet and 11 hosts (5 reserved from 16 available IP addresses) would be available on the AWS VPC.

144-   Your company has assigned you the task for encrypting data in-transit in AWS. Select the ideal design from the following options to complete the given task.

    A. Ensure that security groups and NACLs are configured to address the requirements of the PCI DSS
    B. When using ELB, terminate the TLS connection at the back-end instances
    C. Route egress traffic through a NAT instance
    D. Limit the number of public subnets

Answer: **B**

Explanation: Given below are the design recommendations for encrypting data in transit:

• Consider terminating the TLS links on the Amazon VPC front-end ELB layer or WAF layer and setting up non-TLS links for traffic between private subnets
• Limit the number of public subnets. Public subnets within Amazon VPC are similar to the Demilitarized Zone (DMZ) referred to in the PCI DSS.
• Allow instance-level source / destination controls to provide extra security for network traffic isolation
• Route egress traffic over the Internet via the public subnet's Network Address Translation (NAT) and deploy all other machines on private subnets
• Ensure that PCI DSS requirements are met by security group and NACLs

145- An ELB safety policy is being created by a user. By configuring the server order preference in the security policy of ELB, the user wants ELB to meet the client- supported cipher. Which of the policies listed below would support this feature?

    A. ELBSample- OpenSSLDefault Cipher Policy
    B. ELBDefault Negotiation Policy
    C. ELBSecurity Policy-2011-08
    D. ELBSecurity Policy-2014-01

Answer: **D**
Explanation: The server order preference in AWS is supported by the ELB security policy-2014-01 not by other options.

146- For a cluster computing application, you need the absolute highest network performance. You have already selected homogeneous instance types that support a 10-gigabit enhanced network, ensured the network is linked to your workload and placed instances in a placement group. What is the last optimization that you can make?

    A. Segregate the instances into different peered VPCs while keeping them all in a placement group, so each one has its own Internet Gateway
    B. Create an AMI for the instances and relaunch them, so the instances are fresh in the placement group and do not have noisy neighbors
    C. Use 9001 MTU instead of 1500 for Jumbo Frames, to raise packet body to packet overhead ratios
    D. Turn off SYN/ACK on your TCP stack or begin using UDP for higher throughput

Answer: **C**
Explanation: Jumbo frames allow over 1500 bytes of data, increasing the payload size per packet and thus increasing the packet overhead. Less packets are necessary for sending usable data of the same amount. However, you experience a maximum distance of 1500 MTU outside a given AWS region (EC2-Classic), single VPC, or VPC peering. VPN connections and Internet gateway traffic are restricted to 1500 MTU. If packets are more than 1500 bytes, they are fragmented, or if "No Fragment" flag is set in the IP header, the packet is dropped.

147- Which of these protocols on the Classic Load Balancer is no longer supported for SSL?

    A. TLS 1.2
    B. TLS 1.1
    C. SSL 3.0

D. SSL 2.0

Answer: **D**

Explanation: Versions of SSL protocol supported in AWS are TLS 1.2, TLS 1.1, TLS 1.0 and SSL 3.0.

Deprecated SSL Protocol

We recommend that you update your security policy to the default predefined security policy if you have previously activated the SSL 2.0 protocol within a custom policy.

148-   An EBS-backed EC2 instance was launched by a user. The user started the instance again. In respect of the reboot action, which of the given statement is not true?

   A. The volume is preserved
   B. The private and public address remains the same
   C. The instance runs on a new host computer
   D. The Elastic IP remains associated with the instance

Answer: **C**

Explanation: An instance reboot is similar to an OS reboot. Generally, rebooting takes a few minutes. If you reboot an instance, it will remain on the same physical host so that the instance retains its private IPv4, IPv6 addresses (if applicable), public DNS (IPv4) name and any data in the instance store volumes.

149-   You are implementing CloudHub in AWS for multiple VPN connections. Which of the given options is incorrect?

   A. You need to create a single customer gateway at the main site
   B. AWS CloudHub can be used to provide secure communication between sites
   C. You need to create a Virtual Private Gateway on the AWS side
   D. You need to use the Border gateway protocol

Answer: **A**

Explanation: You can secure communication between sites via the AWS VPN by using multiple VPN connections.

You need to create a Virtual Private Gateway with multiple customer gateways in order to use AWS VPN CloudHub. You have to use a unique Border Gateway Protocol (BGP) Autonomous System Number (ASN) for each customer gateway. Customer gateways advertise the appropriate routes (BGP prefixes) over their VPN connections.

150- Which of the following option is wrong when a link aggregation group is associated with an AWS Direct Connect connection?

A. The connection can be standalone, or it can be a part of another LAG
B. It can be used to aggregate multiple 1 gigabits or 10-gigabit connections at a single AWS Direct Connect endpoint
C. You can associate an existing connection with a LAG
D. The connection can be on a different AWS device

Answer: **D**

Explanation: A Link Aggregation Group is a logical interface using the Link Aggregation Control Protocol (LACP) to add multiple connections of 1 gigabit or 10 gigabits to one AWS Direct Connect connection endpoint, which allows you to treat these connections as a unique, managed connection.

An existing connection can be associated with a LAG. The link can be standalone or part of another LAG. It must be connected to the same AWS device, and the same bandwidth as the LAG must be used. If the connection is already associated with another LAG, you cannot re-associate it if removing the connection causes the original LAG to fall below its threshold for a minimum number of operational connections.

151-An Elastic Load Balancing is configured to enable an SSL (Secure Socket Layer). Negotiation Configuration is known as a Security Policy. In negotiating the SSL connection between the user and the client, which of these options is not a part of this Security Policy?

A. SSL Ciphers
B. SSL Protocols
C. Client Order Preference
D. Server Order Preference

Answer: **C**

Explanation: The SSL protocols, SSL Ciphers and server order preference are all in the predefined policies. There is no customer order preference.

152- Your company is currently distributing content to users via a CloudFront distribution. Which of the following options can be used to ensure that only authorized users get to access content from the distribution? (Choose 2)

A. Configure CloudFront OAI

B. Configure signed cookies

C. Configure Network Access Control Lists

D. Configure an SSL on the distribution

Answer: **A & B**

Explanation: You should generate the CloudFront-signed URLs or signed cookies to restrict access to the documents you serve from Amazon S3 buckets. The CloudFront-Special User will then be created and associated with your allocation, namely the Origin Access Identity (OAI). Then configure permissions so that CloudFront is able to access the OAI and serve your users files, but users cannot use a S3 direct URL to access a file.

153- When comparing NAT instances with NAT gateways, which of the following option is false?

A. The NAT gateways are managed by AWS

B. The bandwidth of NAT gateways supports bursts of up to 10Gbps. For NAT instances, it depends on the instance type

C. NAT gateways are highly available by default

D. You can associate security groups with both the NAT instances and NAT gateways

Answer: **D**

Explanation: You cannot associate a security group with a NAT gateway. However, security groups can be associated with the resources that are behind a NAT gateway for controlling in/outbound traffic.

154- To accessing AWS resources from an EC2 instance, which is the best option to use?

A. Consider implementing IAM Roles

B. Use the root access keys

C. Define an IAM user and use the access keys attached to the user

D. Segregate IAM users into groups

Answer: **A**

Explanation: These use cases are addressed by IAM roles and temporary security credentials. The IAM role allows you to define a set of permissions to access the resources required by a user or service, but the permissions are not attached to a particular IAM user or group. Instead, IAM users, mobiles and EC2-based applications, or AWS services (like Amazon EC2) can programmatically assume a role.

155-   What is the maximum permissible time for connection drain on a Classic Load Balancer?

A. 1 hour
B. 2 hours
C. 3 hours
D. 4 hours

Answer: **A**

Explanation: If you enable the draining of the connection, the load balancer maximum time can be specified to keep the connections alive before reporting the instance as deregistered. The maximum timeout can be set from 1 to 3600 seconds. The load balancing device forcibly closes the load links to the deregistering instance when the maximum time limit is reached.

156-   Select the correct ways to provide additional protective layers for all of your EC2 resources.

A. Add an IP address condition to policies that specify the requests to EC2 instances should come from a specific IP address or CIDR block range
B. Add policies that have deny and/or allow permissions on tagged resources
C. All actions listed here would provide additional layers of protection
D. Ensure that the proper tagging strategies have been implemented to identify all of your EC2 resources

Answer: **B, D**

Explanation: Option D is correct as tagging can help us to understand which resources to test and develop, and check whether production environment is done properly. Tags allow you to categorize your AWS resources in various ways, for example, by purpose, owner, or environment. It is useful if you have many similar resources – you can quickly identify a particular resource based on the tags that you have assigned to them. A key and an optional value are defined for each tag.

Option B is correct because it adds to the top. If you have tagged resources, you can also permit tagging permissions.

157-   What are the 2 types of triggers that can be set up when AWS Config is used to monitor resources?

A. Templates
B. Monitoring
C. Periodic
D. Configuration Changes

Answer: **C & D**

Explanation: Periodic - AWS Config performs rule evaluations at the frequency you select (for example, every 24 hours).

Configuration Changes — when certain types of resources are established, modified or deleted, AWS Config runs rule evaluations.

158- Which of the given options is not correctly stated when regarding security groups that can be defined for EC2 instances?

A. You can specify separate rules for inbound and outbound traffic
B. In security groups, you can define both allow and deny rules
C. Security groups are stateful in nature
D. When you create a security group, it has no inbound rules

Answer: **B**

Explanation: Following are the points regarding security groups:

- There are no inbound rules when you create a security group. Therefore, until you add inbound rules to the security group, no inbound traffic from another host in your instance is allowed
- You can specify rules to allow, but not rules to be denied
- Security groups are stateful— the response traffic for the request from an instance may flow, regardless of inbound security groups rules. Responses to allowed inbound traffic are allowed to flow out, regardless of outbound rules
- The inbound and outbound traffic rules can be set separately

159- Your CTO believes that your account in AWS has been hacked. Suppose your hackers are AWS engineers and they did their utmost to cover their footprints, how can you check if unauthorized access exists and if any changes have been made?

A. By using AWS Config SNS Subscriptions and processing events in real time
B. By using CloudTrail backed up to AWS S3 and Glacier
C. By using AWS Config Timeline forensics

D. By using the CloudTrail Log File Integrity Validation

Answer: D

Explanation: You can use CloudTrail log file validation to determine if the log file has been modified, deleted or unchanged after CloudTrail delivers. This feature is built by means of industry-standard algorithms: SHA-256 with RSA for digital signing and SHA-256 for hashing. This makes it computationally infeasible for CloudTrail log files to be modified, deleted or forged without detection. You can use the AWS CLI to validate the files where they have been delivered by CloudTrail.

In security and forensic investigations, validated log files are invaluable. For example, a validated log file allows you to make a positive statement that the log file itself has not changed or that specific user credentials have carried out specific API activities. The validation process for the integrity of the CloudTrail log file also allows you to know whether a log file has been deleted or changed, or positively asserts that no log files have been sent to your account for a given period of time.

160-   An IT Engineer has created a VPC with CIDR 20.0.0.0/16 using the wizard. For connecting to the user's data center, a public subnet CIDR (20.0.0.0/24) and VPN only subnets CIDR (20.0.1.0/24) are created along with the VPN gateway (vgw-12345). The user's data center has CIDR 172.28.0.0/12. The user also configured a NAT (i-123456) instance to enable VPN subnet traffic to the internet. Which of the options are not valid in this scenario for the entry in the main route table?

A. Destination: 20.0.1.0/24 and Target: i-12345
B. Destination: 172.28.0.0/12 and Target: vgw-12345
C. Destination: 20.0.0.0/16 and Target: local
D. Destination: 0.0.0.0/0 and Target: i-12345

Answer: A

Explanation: The user has not associated the subnet's route table with the main route table because the only route that should have an access to the internet is 0.0.0.0/0. The CIDR 20.0.1.0/24 is VPN only subnet so it does not require an internet access directly via igw.

161-   Select the option that is not part of the logs and can be obtained by requesting Route 53.

A. The domain that was requested
B. DNS Response code

    C. The DNS record type

    D. The client IP address

Answer: **D**

Explanation: Amazon Route 53 can be configured to log information on requests received by Amazon Route 53, such as:

- The Amazon Route 53 edge location that responded to the DNS query
- The date and time of the request
- The DNS response code, such as NoError or ServFail
- The domain or subdomain that was requested
- The DNS record type (such as A or AAAA)

162-   Choose from the following terms that refer to the largest allowed packet to be passed through a network connection.

    A. Maximum connection unit

    B. Maximum transmission unit

    C. Maximum network unit

    D. Maximum received unit

Answer: **B**

Explanation: A network connection's Maximum Transmission Unit (MTU) is the size of the largest permissible packet in bytes that can be passed over the connection. The larger a connection's MTU, the greater the amount of data that can be passed in one packet. Ethernet packets consist of the frame or the actual data you send and the overhead network information surrounding it.

163-   A company has placed a set of on-site resources with an AWS Direct Connect provider. After connecting to a local AWS region in the US. A company requires a connection to S3 public endpoints over the dedicated low latency Direct connect connection. What steps must be taken to make a Direct Connect connection with a public S3 endpoint?

    A. Configure a public virtual interface to connect to a public S3 endpoint resource

    B. Add a BGP route as part of the on-premises router; this will route S3 related traffic to the public S3 endpoint to dedicated AWS region

    C. Establish a VPN connection from the VPC to the public S3 endpoint

   D. Configure a private virtual interface to connect to the public S3 endpoint via the Direct Connect connection

Answer: **A**

Explanation: To start using your AWS Direct Connect connection, you must create a virtual interface. To connect to public resources, you can create a public virtual interface or a private virtual interface to connect to your VPC. Multiple virtual interfaces can be configured on a single AWS Direct Connect connection, and each VPC needs a private virtual interface. Each virtual interface requires a VLAN ID, ASN and BGP key.

164-   From the options mentioned below, which does not belong to the attributes of an Elastic Network Interface?

   A. One or more secondary private IPv4 addresses
   B. One Elastic IP address (IPv4) per public IPv4 address
   C. A primary private IPv4 address
   D. One public IPv4 address

Answer: **B**

Explanation: Given below is the list of network interface attributes:
- A MAC addresses
- One public IPv4 address
- One Elastic IP address (IPv4) per private IPv4 address
- One or more secondary private IPv4 addresses
- A description
- One or more IPv6 addresses
- A source/destination check flag
- One or more security groups
- A primary private IPv4 address

165-   You manage a large company's AWS account. The organization has a workforce of over 1000 and wants to provide most employees with access to different services. Which one is the best possible step to fulfil this requirement?

A. The user should create IAM groups as per the organization's departments and add each user to the group for better access control
B. The user should create a separate IAM user for each employee and provide access to them as per the policy
C. Attach an IAM role with the organization's authentication service to authorize each user for various AWS services
D. The user should create an IAM role and attach STS with the role. The user should attach that role to the EC2 instance and setup AWS authentication on that server

Answer: **C**
Explanation: IAM is best practiced for roles that have specific access to an AWS service and allow users to use the AWS service.

166-   To ensure that you can use alternative domain names with your CloudFront distribution, what should be done?

A. Ensure that you own the domain name and create a CNAME record with the DNS service
B. Ensure the CNAME is created for the zone apex record
C. Ensure that an AAA record is created along with the CNAME record
D. Ensure that a reverse pointer record is created along with the CNAME record

Answer: **A**
Explanation: When you add an alternative domain name to a distribution, you must create a CNAME record on the DNS configuration for routing DNS queries for the domain name in your CloudFront distribution.

167-   In the comparison of NAT instances with NAT gateways, which of the following statement is false?

A. The NAT gateways are managed by AWS
B. You can associate security groups with both the NAT instances and NAT gateways
C. The bandwidth of NAT gateways supports bursts of up to 10Gbps, and NAT instances depends on the instance type
D. NAT gateways are highly available by default

Answer: **B**

Explanation:

A NAT gateway cannot be linked to security groups. To monitor inbound and outbound traffic, connect security groups to your assets behind the NAT gateway.

168- For Multiple IP addressing in AWS, indicate the false statement.

    A. Security groups apply to network interfaces, not to IP addresses. Therefore, IP addresses are subject to the security group of the network interface in which they are specified

    B. You can assign a secondary private IPv4 address to any network interface

    C. You can assign multiple IPv6 addresses to a network interface that is in a subnet having an associated IPv6 CIDR block

    D. Multiple IP addresses can only be assigned to network interfaces on stopped instances

Answer: D

Explanation:

- Multiple IP addresses can be assigned and unassigned to network interfaces attached to running or stopped instances

- Multiple IPv6 addresses can be assigned to a network interface in a subnet with an IPv6 CIDR block

- Security groups do not apply to IP addresses but to network interfaces

- For the network interface, you must select the secondary IPv4 from the subnet's IPv4 CIDR block range

- Any network interface can be assigned a secondary private IPv4 address. The network interface can be attached to the instance or removed from it

169- You want to host a subnet in a VPC. Which of the following types you cannot host in a VPC?

    A. Direct Connect Only

    B. VPN only

    C. Public

    D. Private

Answer: A

Explanation: Types of subnets that can be configured:

- VPN - only - You can create a VPN connection between your VPC and your own data center by attaching a Virtual Private Gateway to your VPC
- Private subnets - For private subnets, Internet traffic can be transmitted via a special Network Address Translation (NAT)
- Public Subnet - To set up a public subnet, you must configure your routing table so that traffic from that subnet to the Internet is routed via an Internet gateway linked to the VPC

170- Currently, your private subnets contain EC2 instances. In these instances, there are applications based on IPv6. Your IT manager suggested you to configure NAT instances of public subnet in order to ensure that the hosted applications on private subnet instances can download the required updates. However, the apps can still not download the updates after the instances have been configured. What could be the underlying problem from the following options?

    A. The NAT instance should not be configured in the public subnet; it should be configured in the private subnet

    B. NAT is not supported for IPv6 traffic

    C. The NAT instance is not configured with a private DNS name

    D. The NAT instance is not configured with a private IP address

Answer: **B**

Explanation: For IPv6 traffic, NAT is not supported therefore, use an egress only internet gateway.

171-You have launched instances into a VPC. Now, the requirement is to receive a DNS hostname and ensure that DNS resolution is possible by using Amazon DNS. Which of the following attributes would you select? (Choose 2)

    A. setDnsHostnames

    B. enableDnsresolution

    C. enableDnsHostnames

    D. enableDnsSupport

Answer: **C & D**

Explanation: Your VPC has attributes that determine if your instance receives public DNS hostnames and whether the Amazon DNS server supports DNS resolution.

- enableDnsSupport - Specifies whether the VPC supports the DNS resolution
- enableDnsHostnames - Specifies whether the instances launched in the VPC receive public DNS hostnames

172- You are running an EC2 instance that is hosting a web server. The given table is the NACL attached to the subnet hosting the EC2 instances.

Rule #	Type	Protocol	Port Range	Destination	Allow/ Deny
100	HTTP (80)	TCP (6)	80	10.1.0.0/16	ALLOW
101	HTTPS (443)	TCP (6)	443	10.1.0.0/16	ALLOW
200	HTTP (80)	TCP (6)	80	0.0.0.0/0	DENY
201	HTTPS (443)	TCP (6)	443	0.0.0.0/0	DENY
1000	ALL	ALL	ALL	0.0.0.0/0	ALLOW
*	All Traffic	ALL	ALL	0.0.0.0/0	DENY

If port 80 receives a request from the internet to the web server, what will happen?

A. The request will be allowed because of Rule no 1000, which matches the request
B. The request will be denied because of Rule no *
C. The request will be allowed because of Rule no 100, which matches the request
D. The request will be denied because of Rule no 200

Answer: **C**

Explanation: Rules shall be assessed beginning with the lowest numbered rule.

The rule applies as soon as it matches the traffic, irrespective of any higher numbered rule that might conflict with that rule. As a packet enters the subnet, we evaluate it according to the ACL rules with which the subnet (from the top of the rules list and to the bottom) is associated. This is the way the assessment takes place if the packet is for the SSL port (443). The first rule (Rule 100) is not the same as that of the packet. The second rule (110) enables the packet to enter the subnet. The rule ultimately denies that packet, if the packet had been designated for port 139 (NetBIOS) and does not match any of the rules.

173- Choose the following annotation which is normally referred to when BGP is used for autonomous routing.

A. iBGP
B. eBGP

C. sBGP

D. pBGP

Answer: **A**

Explanation: BGP can be used in an autonomous system for routing. It is referred to as the Interior Border Gateway Protocol, Internal BGP or iBGP in this application. The Internet application of the protocol may be referred to as the External Border Gateway Protocol, External BGP or eBGP

174-   You are working in a company that is in charge of the VPN connection between the on-site data center and AWS. This VPN connection must be monitored to notify you when the connection is down. What steps should the take to fulfill the requirement? (Choose 2)

A. Ensure that the CloudWatch log being monitored is TunnelState for the VPN connection

B. Ensure that CloudWatch metric being monitored is TunnelState for the VPN connection

C. Create a CloudWatch log

D. Create a CloudWatch alarm that sends a notification whenever the state of the alarm is set to ALARM

Answer: **B & D**

Explanation: You can monitor the status of an AWS VPN through its metric data, which is automatically sent to CloudWatch. The VPN tunnel state is reported as a Boolean value in the CloudWatch metric TunnelState. After setting up VPN and tunnels, you can configure CloudWatch alarms to monitor the connection.

175-   For end-to-end security, IPSec protocol is used. Which of the following Internet protocol layer is suitable for this purpose?

A. Transport Layer

B. Link Layer

C. Application Layer

D. Internet Layer

Answer: **D**

Explanation: IPsec is an end-to-end IP Layer security scheme whereas other internet security systems like Transport Layer Security (TLS) and Secure Shell (SSH) operate in high layers of the Transport Layer (TLS) and Application Layer (SSH), which are commonly known to be used in Internet Layers. IPsec can secure applications on the IP layer automatically.

176-   Given below is the list of Direct Connect and VPN connections of your company.

- Site A - VPN 10.1.0.0/28 AS 65000 65000
- Site B - VPN 10.1.0.252/24 AS 65000
- Site C - Direct Connect 10.0.0.0/8 AS 65000
- Site D - Direct Connect 10.0.0.0/16 AS 65000 65000 65000

Which of the site will AWS use to reach to your network?

A. Site A
B. Site B
C. Site C
D. Site D

Answer: **A**

Explanation: AWS uses the most specific route in your route table to match traffic to determine how traffic is routed (longest matching prefix). We can see that Site A has the longest prefix that is /28.

177-   You want to connect multiple VPCs in various AWS regions and to do that, you have the following options. Which option do you think is not applicable?

A. Ensure you implement a Highly Available (HA) design
B. Ensure that your VPC network ranges (CIDR blocks) do not overlap
C. Use network equipment that supports IPSec VPN tunnels and Border Gateway Protocol
D. You should try to connect all VPCs

Answer: **D**

Explanation: There are some universal principles of network design to consider when connecting multiple VPCs in different AWS regions:

- Make sure your VPC network ranges (CIDR blocks) do not overlap
- Ensure that the solution you choose is able to scale according to your current and future VPC connectivity requirements

- Ensure that a Highly Available (HA) design is implemented without a single fault point
- Consider your data transfer needs, since this affects your choice of solution. Based on the amount of information transmitted, some solutions offered below may prove to be costlier than others
- When applicable, use network equipment supporting IPSec VPN tunnels and Border Gateway Protocol (BGP)
- Connect only the VPCs that really need to communicate

178- A company is establishing Virtual interfaces in AWS. Which of the following options is not required for this purpose?

    A. An ASN for the BGP Session
    B. Peer IP Address
    C. BGP multi-exit discriminator
    D. VLAN ID

Answer: **C**

Explanation: For a virtual interface, the following information is required:

- <u>BGP Information</u>: For your side of the BGP session, a virtual interface must have a public or private Border Gateway Protocol (BGP) Autonomous System Number (ASN)
- <u>Peer IP addresses</u>: The range of IP addresses assigned for the BGP peering session at each end of the virtual interface
- <u>VLAN</u>: Each virtual interface must be tagged with a new, unused customer provided tag (VLAN ID) that meets the Ethernet 802.1Q standard

179- Your Company has assigned you the task of load balancing setup in AWS by using HTTPS for the back-end instances and path-based routing. Which of the Load Balancer would you choose?

    A. Network Load Balancer
    B. Application Load Balancer
    C. Secondary Load Balancer
    D. Classic Load Balancer

Answer: **B**

Explanation: Some of the Application Load Balancer's key points over the Classic Load Balancer are:

- Path-based routing support. You can set rules that forward requests based on the URL in the request for your listener. This allows you to structure your application as smaller services and route requests to the correct service based on the content of the URL

- Host-based routing support. You can set rules for your listener to forward requests in the HTTP header based on the host field. This allows you to use a single load balancer to route requests to multiple domains

180- In order to mark the record of any activity, which of the CloudTrail component is suitable?

    A. CloudTrail Events
    B. CloudTrail Logs
    C. CloudTrail Alarms
    D. CloudTrail Workflow

Answer: **A**

Explanation: A CloudTrail event is the record of an AWS account activity. This activity can be an action taken by a user, role or service that can be monitored by CloudTrail. CloudTrail events provide a history of API and non-API account activities via the AWS Management Console, AWS SDKs, command line tools and other AWS services.

181- Choose 3 services from the following options which are most feasible to be used in conjunction with CloudWatch Logs.

    A. Amazon SQS
    B. Amazon Lambda
    C. Amazon Kinesis
    D. Amazon S3

Answer: **B, C, & D**

Explanation: The products that can be integrated with CloudWatch logs are:

- Amazon S3 - To store your log data in highly durable storage such as S3, you can use CloudWatch Logs

- Amazon Lambda - The functions of Lambda can work with CloudWatch logs

- Amazon Kinesis - Data for real-time analysis can be fed here

182- You create an application that stores highly sensitive financial data. All system information must be encrypted during rest and transit. What could breach this policy?

    A. CloudFront Viewer Protocol Policy set to HTTPS redirection

    B. ELB Using Proxy Protocol v1

    C. ELB SSL termination

    D. Telling S3 to use AES256 on the server-side

Answer: **C**

Explanation: When you use SSL termination, your servers will always get insecure connections and never know whether or not users used a secured channel.

183- Organization has an on-premises environment having a DNS server and active directory for authentication. You tried to fix the on-premises resources through the EC2 instances in AWS VPC, but this does not work. What might be the reason behind this? (Choose 2)

    A. The Security Group is blocking port 80 inbound

    B. The NACL is blocking UDP port 53 outbound

    C. The Security Group is blocking port 80 outbound

    D. The NACL is blocking TCP port 53 outbound

Answer: **B & D**

Explanation: Port 53 is the network ports of a DNS server. Therefore, in the Network Access Control Lists, these ports must be opened for output.

DNS messages are transmitted between DNS servers or between DNS server from DNS clients during DNS resolution. Both UDP and DNS servers bind messages to UDP port 53. If the length of the message is higher than that of a User Datagram Protocol (UDP) datagram (512 octets), the first reply will be given with the maximum number of data available on the UDP datagram; then the DNS Server will set a flag that indicates the truncated answer. The sender of the message may then reissue the query to the DNS server via TCP (TCP port 53).

184- Which of this can be used to limit traffic to your VPC subnets?

    A. VPC Flow Logs

B. Network Access Control Lists

C. Subnet Security Groups

D. Security Groups

Answer: **B**

Explanation: AWS offers two features to enhance security in your VPC: security groups and network ACLs. Inbound and outbound traffic are controlled by security groups for your instances, and network ACLs monitor inbound and outbound traffic in your subnets.

185-   Which of the following CloudFront requests will not directly return the request to the source server?

A. GET

B. OPTIONS

C. POST

D. PUT

Answer: **A**

Explanation: Other methods will return the request to the origin server directly. The GET application allows for contents to be checked first at the edge locations. When there is no content, the request is sent for the content to the origin server. It will not directly return the request.

186-   You want to run Microsoft Active Directory (AD) as a managed service. Which of the following services will you use?

A. Amazon Cloud Directory

B. Simple AD

C. AD Connector

D. AWS Directory Service

Answer: **D**

Explanation: You can run the Microsoft Active Directory as a managed service by AWS Directory Service. AWS Directory Service for Microsoft Active Directory, also referred to as Microsoft AD, is powered by Windows Server 2012 R2. When this directory type is selected and launched, it is made as a highly available pair of domain controllers connected to your VPC. In a region of your choice, the domain controllers run in different availability zones. Host monitoring

and recovery, data replication, snapshots, and software updates are automatically configured and managed for you.

187-   A subnet with 10.0.1.0/24 CIDR block is provided and you launch an EC2 instance in it. From the following options, which option cannot be assigned as an IP address?

   A. 10.0.1.253
   B. 10.0.1.4
   C. 10.0.1.254
   D. 10.0.1.3

Answer: **D**

Explanation: You cannot assign the initial four IP addresses and the last IP address for each CIDR block subnet. For example, the following five IP addresses are reserved for a subnet with CIDR block 10.0.0.0/24:

- 10.0.0.0: Network address
- 10.0.0.1: Reserved by AWS for the VPC router
- 10.0.0.2: Reserved by AWS. The IP address of the DNS server is always the base of the VPC network range plus two; however, we also reserve the base of each subnet range plus two
- 10.0.0.3: Reserved by AWS for future use
- 10.0.0.255: Network broadcast address. AWS does not support broadcast in a VPC. Therefore, we reserve this address

188-   A Direct Connect connection to AWS is currently available to your company. Users have to work with S3 buckets directly. Private EC2 servers must also have access to S3 content. Which of these can be used to fulfill this requirement?

   A. A Virtual Private Gateway
   B. A Public Virtual Interface
   C. A Private Virtual Interface
   D. A Hosted Virtual Interface

Answer: **B & C**

Explanation: Use a public virtual interface to connect with AWS public endpoints (e.g., Amazon EC2 or Amazon S3) with dedicated network performance

A private virtual interface is used to connect to private services, including a dedicated Amazon VPC network performance

189- Your company has assigned you the task to monitor different users and entities. You must also monitor the API calls against AWS account. A history of those calls will be required for a later review. Which services would you select for this task?

    A. AWS CloudTrail: CloudWatch Events
    B. AWS CloudTrail: AWS Config
    C. AWS Config: AWS Lambda
    D. AWS Config: AWS Inspector

Answer: **A**

Explanation: You can use AWS CloudTrail to access your account with a history of AWS API calls and associated events. API calls that are made while using the AWS Management Console, AWS Command Line Interface, AWS SDK's and other AWS services are included in this history.

Amazon CloudWatch Events provide an infinite number of system events that describe changes in the resources of Amazon Web Services (AWS). You can match and route events to one or more target functions or streams using simple rules that you can set quickly. Operational changes are noticed in CloudWatch Events. In response to such changes, CloudWatch Events send messages in order to react to the environment, activate functions, change, and capture state information and apply corrections when necessary.

190- What can be used to connect your AWS Direct Connect connection to one or more VPCs on your account, in the same region or in different regions, via a private virtual interface?

    A. AWS Direct Connect Interface
    B. AWS Direct Connect Gateway
    C. AWS Direct Connect Connector
    D. AWS Direct Connect Replicator

Answer: **B**

Explanation: You can use a gateway to connect your AWS Direct Connect to one or more of the VPCs on your account in the same or different regions via a private virtual interface. You combine a Direct Connect Gateway with the VPC's virtual private gateway and then create an AWS Direct Connect Private Virtual Interface with the Direct Connect Gateway. A number of private virtual interfaces can be attached to your direct connection gateway.

191- Choose 3 options, which are network requirements to establish a Direct Connect connection.

    A. Support Border Gateway Protocol (BGP)

    B. Connections to AWS Direct Connect require Single Mode Fiber, 1000BASE-LX (1310nm) for 1 Gigabit Ethernet

    C. Support for AES Encryption

    D. Support for BGP MD5 authentication

Answer: **A, B, & D**

Explanation: In order to use AWS Direct Connect from an AWS Direct Connect location, one of the following given conditions is required for your network:

- You must work with AWS Direct Connect, an AWS Partner Network (APN) member. To connect to AWS Direct Connect, you must work with independent service providers

- Your network must collocated with an existing AWS Direct Connect location

Moreover, the following conditions must apply to your network:

- The AWS Direct Connect connections require Single Mode Fiber, 1000BASE - LX (1310 nm) or 10GBASE - LR (1310 nm) for 10 gigabits of Ethernet. Ethernet connections must be single. Port Auto Negotiation has to be deactivated. Through these connections, you need to support 802.1Q VLANs

- BGP and BGP MD5 authentication should be supported by your network

192- A company is running 2 instances (c4.large) in a VPC. For a better network communication between the instances, you decide to create a placement group in which you have to move the created instances. You faced an issue during this. From the following option which might be the issue?

    A. The type of instance is not supported in the placement group

    B. You cannot have instances with EBS volumes in a placement group

    C. You cannot move an existing instance into a placement group

    D. You cannot have Linux Instances in a placement group

Answer: **C**

Explanation:

An existing instance cannot be transferred into a placement group. You can create an AMI from your instance and then start a new instance in a placement group from that AMI.

193- Your security officer suggested you to tighten up the logging of all events that occur on your AWS account because many of your EC2 services go offline once in a week for no reason. He demanded the access for all events occurred in all regions in the easiest and fastest way, and he also mentioned that he should be the only person to have this access. From the following options, which is the best solution for the mentioned requirements?

A. Use CloudTrail to send all API calls to CloudWatch and send an email to the security officer every time an API call is made. Make sure the emails are encrypted

B. Use CloudTrail to log all events to an Amazon Glacier Vault. Make sure the vault access policy only grants access to the security officer's IP address

C. Use CloudTrail to log all events to one S3 bucket. Make this S3 bucket only accessible by your security officer with a bucket policy that restricts access to user only and also adds MFA to the policy for a further level of security

D. Use CloudTrail to log all events to a separate S3 bucket in each region as CloudTrail cannot write to a bucket in a different region. Use MFA and bucket policies on all the different buckets

Answer: **C**

Explanation: Option A is invalid because CloudTrail is needed to monitor the API calls. CloudTrail is not used to send API calls

Option B is not correct because Glacier is not the ideal security officer recall option.

Option D is invalid as it is not ideal for accessing a single security officer using different buckets. CloudTrail can supply log calls to a single S3 bucket. So log all events to single S3 bucket, use CloudTrail. Make this S3 bucket available to security personnel only by using a bucket policy that restricts access to its customer only. For an extra level of security, add MFA as well.

194- Which of the following options provide a detailed list of the IP ranges assigned to and used by AWS?

A. There is no list. You need to contact AWS support for this

B. aws.json

C. ip-ranges.json

D. aws-vpc.json

Answer: C

Explanation: The current IP address ranges of Amazon Web Services (AWS) is published in JSON. Download the ipranges.json file to view the current ranges. Save a successive version of .json file on your system to maintain history. To determine if changes have occurred since the last time the file has been saved, check the time of publication in the current file and compare it with the time of publication for your last file.

195- Your company has a VPC and subnets in AWS, and they have routes for traffic in CIDR 0.0.0.0/0 block for traffic. The company has asked you to establish communication across all hosts, you noticed that IPv6 based applications across subnets in VPC are working improperly. What should you do to resolve this issue?

    A. Add a route for ::/0 to the route table as well

    B. Ensure that the route of 0.0.0.0/0 is removed and a more specific route is placed

    C. Add the default route of 172.132.0.0/16 to the Route table

    D. Remove the route of 0.0.0.0/0 and add the route of ::/0 instead to allow all communication

Answer: A

Explanation: The IPv4 and IPv6 CIDR blocks are treated independently. For example, not all IPv6 addresses are automatically included in a route with a CIDR 0.0.0.0/0 destination (all IPv4 addresses). For all IPv6 addresses, you need to create a route with ::/0 destination.

196- You try to connect to your instance from the internet and get an error message "Network error: Connection timed out or Error connecting to [instance], reason: -> Connection timed out: connect".

Choose 2 options that will enable you to troubleshoot the error.

    A. Check if a private IP address has been assigned to the instance

    B. Check the inbound Security Group Rules

    C. Check the route table for the VPC

    D. Check if the instance has been assigned a private DNS name

Answer: B & C

Explanation:

For troubleshooting EC2 instances connectivity, given below are the steps to follow:

- Check the route table for the subnet. You need a route that sends all traffic destined outside the VPC to the internet gateway for the VPC
- Check your security group rules. You need a security group rule that allows inbound traffic from your public IPv4 address on the proper port

197- Using the VPC wizard, a user has created a public and private subnet in VPC. In this scenario, which of the following statements is false?

    A. The VPC will create one internet gateway and attach it to VPC
    B. The VPC will launch one NAT instance with an elastic IP
    C. The VPC will create a routing instance and attach it with a public subnet
    D. The VPC will create two subnets

Answer: **C**

Explanation: By using the VPC wizard, when you have a private and public subnet, following are created:

- One NAT instance to route traffic from the public to private subnet
- 2 subnets – one private and one public
- One internet gateway attached to the VPC

198- You have an obligation to create a subnet that can host 2000 addresses. Which of the network masks would you use to ensure that it is as accurate as possible to host required number of IP addresses?

    A. /21
    B. /22
    C. /23
    D. /24

Answer: **B**

Explanation: If you use different network masks, you can use any online CIDR calculator to see the number of subnets and host addresses. /21 means (32-21=11) 2^{11} = 2048, so 2048 IP addresses are available.

199- An organization's AWS audit is held, for which auditor requires read-only access to all the resources in AWS, logs of VPCs, and events that occurred in AWS account. From the following options which is the best way to provide this access?

    A. Create a role that has the required permissions

    B. Create an SNS notification that sends the CloudTrail log files

    C. Enable CloudTrail logging and create an IAM user who has read-only permissions to the required AWS resources, including the bucket containing the CloudTrail logs

    D. One should contact AWS as part of the shared responsibility model, and AWS will grant the required access

Answer: **C**

Explanation: AWS CloudTrail is used to record user actions by the history of AWS API calls from your account. API calls are made through the management console, SDK or command line. These API calls include the identity of the caller, request parameters, the name of the API, time of the API and responses by AWS service.

The purpose of CloudTrail is to enable security analysis and track changes to your account, and provide compliance auditing.

200- For some EC2 instances, you want to monitor the network interfaces. Which of the given options would help you in this requirement? (Choose 2)

    A. Log into the EC2 instances and choose the networking interfaces

    B. Enable Flow Logs

    C. Go to the necessary network interfaces in the AWS console.

    D. Enable Network interface logging

Answer: **B & C**

Explanation: VPC Flow Logs is a feature that allows you to capture IP traffic information from and to your VPC's network interfaces. Flow Log data are stored via Amazon CloudWatch Logs. You can view and retrieve your data in Amazon CloudWatch logs after you have created a Flow Log. You can also go to specific network interface via console to monitor it.

201- What is the term for networks presenting a clearly defined external internet routing policy?

    A. Autonomous System Locators

B. Autonomous System Numbers
C. Internet System Locators
D. Internet System Numbers

Answer: **B**

Explanation: To identify networks with a clearly defined external routing policy to the Internet, autonomous system numbers are used. AWS Direct Connect requires the creation of a virtual public or private interface by using ASN. You can use a public ASN you own, or you can choose between 64512 and 65535 for any private ASN number.

202- You are working in a company that has a stateless web application with the below mentioned components:

- A MySQL RDS database with 2000 provisioned IOPS
- An Elastic Load Balancer
- 4 Web/Application servers on EC2

The CPU utilization of the database server is 20% while the web server is around 92% shown by the CloudWatch metrics. Which of the 2 options below can be used to reduce the load of the entire infrastructure?

A. Make use of auto-scaling and launch more Web/Application servers
B. Create a read replica for the database
C. Consider increasing the instance type of the Web/Application Servers
D. Enable Multi-AZ for the database

Answer: **A & C**

Explanation: As the load on the Web / Application servers is high, the use of auto-scaling and an increase in the number or type of instance of current Web / Application servers should be considered. In this way, the load is balanced on web/application servers.

203- In the same availability zone, a VPC is created with two EC2 instances in different subnets. One instance is to run the database while the other instance is for an application to interface with database. You have to confirm the communication between them for working of your application. Choose two options to apply in VPC settings in order to confirm communication between EC2 instances.

A. The default route is set to a NAT instance or an Internet GateWay (IGW) for them to communicate

B. Security groups are set to allow the application host to talk to the database on the right port/protocol

C. A network ACL that allows communication between the two subnets

D. Both instances are the same instance class and use the same key-pair

Answer: **B & C**

Explanation:

The security groups must be defined to allow the web server to communicate to the database server whenever you design the web server and database server. NACL is also need to be define for both subnet communications.

204-   Identify the incorrect statement about AWS Direct Connect in the given options.

A. Each connection can be used across multiple AWS regions

B. Both the 1-gigabit or 10-gigabit speed options are available

C. It can help have a consistent network performance

D. It is a private connection that is separate from the internet

Answer: **A**

Explanation: AWS Direct Connect connects your internal network via the standard 1 Gb or 10 Gb Ethernet fiber - optic cable to an AWS Direct Connect location. One end of the cable is connected to the AWS Direct Connect Router, and the other is connected to your router. This connection enables the creation of virtual interfaces directly to public AWS services (for example, to Amazon S3) or to Amazon VPC, bypassing Internet service providers in your network path. An AWS Direct Connect location provides access to AWS in the region with which it is associated, and you can use a single connection in a public region or AWS GovCloud (US) to access public AWS services in all other public regions.

205-   In order to automate network creation using CloudFormation, which of the following types of private IP address would be assigned?

A. AWS::EC2::VPC

B. AWS::EC2::SubnetCidrBlock

C. AWS::EC2::Subnet

D. AWS::EC2::NetworkInterface

Answer: D

Explanation: This would be the network interface. An example is given below:

```
{
    "AWSTemplateFormatVersion" : "2010-09-09",
    "Description" : "Simple Standalone ENI",
    "Resources" : {
        "myENI" : {
            "Type" : "AWS::EC2::NetworkInterface",
            "Properties" : {
            "Tags": [{"Key":"foo","Value":"bar"}],
            "Description": "A nice description.",
            "SourceDestCheck": "false",
            "GroupSet": ["sg-75zzz219"],
            "SubnetId": "subnet-3z648z53",
            "PrivateIpAddress": "10.0.0.16"
            }
        }
    }
}
```

206-   You decided to establish VPC peering connection on two VPCs, i.e., VPCA (172.16.0.0/16) and VPCB (10.0.0.0/16). Choose 2 routes from the given options that should be added in the route table for both VPCs in order to establish communication between VPCs, assuming that the ID pcx-1122 is assigned to the VPC peering connection.

   A. In the Route table for VPCB, add a route of 10.0.0.0/16 and Target as pcx-1122
   B. In the Route table for VPCA, add a route of 172.16.0.0/16 and Target as pcx-1122
   C. In the Route table for VPCB, add a route of 172.16.0.0/16 and Target as pcx-1122
   D. In the Route table for VPCA, add a route of 10.0.0.0/16 and Target as pcx-1122

Answer: **C & D**

Explanation: To send traffic from a VPC to its peered VPC; you must add routes in the route tables of both the VPCs. In VPC A, you need to add route for VPC B and for VPC B, add route for VPC A.

207-   Your company has resources in on-premises and AWS. You are working there as a Network Administrator. You want to create a VPN connection between on-premises infrastructure and AWS; management should be enabled on both sides. Which of the given options would facilitate you for this requirement? (Choose 2)

    A. Use Direct Connect as the connectivity option
    B. Use a software VPN appliance in your VPC
    C. Create a customer gateway on the on-premises location
    D. Use the amazon virtual private interface

Answer: **B & C**
Explanation: You can fully manage both sides of your Amazon VPC connectivity by establishing a VPN link between your remote network and a VPN appliance software that works on your Amazon VPC network. Your remote network must have customer gateway for VPN connectivity. This option is suggested if both ends of the VPN connection are managed for compliance reasons or for the exploitation of non-Amazon VPC support gateway systems.

208-   A company has established Direct Connect between its on-site location and its AWS VPC. In the event when the Direct Connect fails, they wish to setup redundancy. In this respect, what can they do? Select all applicable options.

    A. Setup S3 connection
    B. Setup another Direct Connect connection
    C. Setup an IPSec VPN connection
    D. Setup a connection via EC2 instances

Answer: **B & C**
Explanation: If a second AWS Direct Connect connection has been established, traffic will automatically failover to the second link. When configured to ensure fast detection and failure, we recommend Bidirectional Forwarding Detection (BFD) for your connections. If you have set up an IPsec VPN backup connection instead, the VPN connection will automatically fail to be connected to any VPC traffic. Traffic will be routed via the Internet to/from public sources like Amazon S3. If you do not have an AWS Direct Connect backup link or an IPsec VPN link, in the

event of a failure, Amazon VPC traffic will be dropped. Public resources traffic will be routed through the internet.

209- You want to use Simple AD for resolving names using DNS servers within VPC and outside VPC. Which of the following options will allow you to do this task?

    A. DNSName Resolution
    B. Route 53
    C. DHCP Options Set
    D. DNSNameSet

Answer: **C**

Explanation: If you want your Simple AD to resolve names using both DNS servers in your VPC and private DNS servers outside your VPC, you can do so by using a set of DHCP options.

210- Which type of record set cannot be created for a private hosted zone in Route 53?

    A. Geolocation
    B. Simple
    C. Failover
    D. Weighted

Answer: **A**

Explanation: Following Routing Policies can be used while creating the record set in the private hosted zone:

- Simple
- Failover
- Weighted

211- Which of the following port/protocol is used by the Amazon Workspaces for Authentication?

    A. TCP/80
    B. UDP/443
    C. HTTP/80
    D. HTTPS/443

Answer: **D**

Explanation: Clients utilize port 443 of HTTPS for all the session related information and authentication in Amazon Workspace.

212-   In an AWS setup, you have the requirement to monitor the traffic that is being directed to the CloudFront setup. Which service can be used for this purpose?

    A. AWS Shield

    B. AWS CloudFront Logs

    C. AWS WAF

    D. AWS CloudWatch

Answer: **C**

Explanation: AWS WAF is a web application firewall that helps you monitor the HTTP and HTTPS requests that are forwarded to Amazon CloudWatch and an Application Load Balancer.

213-   Which of the following record types in Route 53 can be used for IPv6 addresses?

    A. A

    B. AAAA

    C. CNAME

    D. PTR

Answer: **B**

Explanation: The value for an AAAA record is an IPV6 address in colon-separated hexadecimal format.

214-   On Classic Load Balancer, which of the following setting helps in defining the amount of time between the health checks of an individual backend instance?

    A. Health Check Interval

    B. Unhealthy Threshold

    C. Response Timeout

    D. Healthy Threshold

Answer: **A**

Explanation: The Health Check Interval is the amount of the time between the health checks of an individual instance.

215-   To ensure that the same set of name servers are used across multiple domains in Route 53, what would be your strategy?

    A. Create a delegation set via the console
    B. Create a dual hosted zone in Route 53
    C. Create a delegation set via the AWS CLI
    D. Create a primary hosted zone in Route 53

Answer: **C**

Explanation: By default, each hosted zone that you create gets a different set of four name servers—a different delegation set. If you create a lot of hosted zones, maintaining different delegation sets can be difficult and time-consuming. Route 53 lets you create a delegation set via AWS CLI that you can reuse with multiple hosted zones.

216-   Choose two correct statements about the default Network ACL assigned to the default VPC.

    A. The Network ACL inbound rules allow all traffic
    B. The Network ACL inbound rules deny all traffic
    C. The Network ACL outbound rules allow all traffic
    D. The Network ACL outbound rules deny all traffic

Answer: **A & C**

Explanation: The default Network ACL is configured to allow all site visitors to float inside and out of the subnets with which it is far related. Each Network ACL also includes a rule whose rule number is an asterisk. This rule ensures that if a packet does not match any of the other numbered rules, it is denied. You cannot modify or remove this rule.

217-   A business-to-business web application, which is running in a VPC consists of ELB, web servers, application servers, and databases. Your web application only accepts the traffic from a pre-defined customer IP addresses. Which options will fulfill this requirement? (Choose 2)

    A. Configure web servers VPC security groups to allow traffic from your customer's IPs

B. Configure your web servers to filter traffic based on the ELBs "X-forwarded for" header

C. Configure ELB security groups to allow traffic from your customer's IPs and deny all outbound traffic

D. Configure a VPC NACL to allow web traffic from your customer's IPs and deny all outbound traffic

Answer: A & B

Explanation: The Web Servers Security Groups help ensure that requests come from the IPs of customers via the rules in the security groups. The X-forwarded-for request header helps to identify the IP address of the client when you use an HTTP and HTTPS load balancer.

218- To optimize the performance of compute-cluster that requires low inter-node latency, which feature should be used?

A. AWS Direct Connect

B. AWS Placement Group

C. VPC Private Subnets

D. EC2 Dedicated Instances

E. Multiple Availability Zones

Answer: B

Explanation: A placement group is the logical grouping of the instances within a single AZ. They are recommended for the applications that have low network latencies, high network throughputs or both. To provide the higher performance and low latency for your placement group, choose the instance type which supports enhanced networking.

219- You have servers in your VPC within a private subnet that requires to access the internet. Select the highly available solution.

A. Convert the subnet to a public subnet

B. Deploy a NAT instance

C. Deploy a bastion host

D. Use the NAT gateway service

Answer: D

Explanation: Since, high availability is required, it is preferred to use the NAT gateway option for providing an internet access to private subnet in VPC.

220- Which of the following services can be used along with the AWS WAF service? (Choose 2)

    A. AWS SQS
    B. AWS ELB
    C. AWS CloudFront
    D. AWS Lambda

Answer: **B & C**

Explanation: AWS WAF is used to control the AWS CloudFront and Application Load Balancer's respond to the web requests. This starts by creating rules, conditions, and web ACLs. You create your condition, combine them with the set of rules and attach them with web ACL.

221- CloudFront provides the URLs, and you want to add the expiration date in these URLs. How can you do this?

    A. By setting an expiration date for the CloudFront distribution. This would then add the same date to the URLs
    B. By using a signed URL
    C. By using cookies to embed the expiration date
    D. This is not possible with CloudFront

Answer: **B**

Explanation: Signed URL includes the additional information. For example, an expiration date and time which provides you with more control and access to your content.

222- Logs are enabled for a Classic Load Balancer, and there is a need to perform the SQL queries on the log files. Which actions would you perform? (Choose 2)

    A. Configure the logs to be copied to S3
    B. Configure the logs to be copied to Athena
    C. Use the Athena service to query the logs
    D. Use the EMR service to query the logs

Answer: **A & C**

Explanation: Amazon Athena is a very interactive query service that makes it easy to analyze the data in Amazon S3 using the standard SQL. So initially, ensure that logs are copied to S3 and for analyzing, use Athena.

223- What is the name of the label, applied to the packets that allow the router to know where to forward these packets in an MPLS network?

   A. BFD
   B. BGP
   C. DSCP
   D. FEC

Answer: **D**

Explanation: A Forwarding Equivalence Class (FEC) is a term used in Multiprotocol Label Switching (MPLS) to describe a set of packets with similar or identical characteristics that may be forwarded the same way; that is, they may be bound to the same MPLS label.

224- To create a VPC Flow Logs, which of the following options are required? (Choose 3)

   A. The resource for which the log needs to be created
   B. An IAM role with the privilege to publish the logs to CloudWatch
   C. A CloudWatch log group
   D. A CloudWatch log stream

Answer: **A, B, & C**

Explanation: To create a Flow Log, you specify the resource for which you want to create the Flow Log, the type of traffic to capture (accepted traffic, rejected traffic, or all traffic), the name of a log group in CloudWatch Logs to which the Flow Log will be published, and the ARN of an IAM role that has sufficient permission to publish the Flow Log to the CloudWatch Logs log group.

225- Which of the following is not a protocol that is used when monitoring an endpoint using Route 53 health checks?

   A. HTTP
   B. HTTPS

    C. TCP

    D. UDP

Answer: **D**

Explanation: Amazon Route 53 use HTTP, HTTPS and TCP to check the health of the endpoints.

226- Which three types of health checks are monitored using Route 53 Health Check? (Choose 3)

    A. Health checks that monitor an endpoint

    B. Health checks that monitor CloudWatch Alarms

    C. Health checks that monitor CloudWatch Logs

    D. Health checks that monitor other health checks

Answer: **A, B, & D**

Explanation: Three types of Amazon Route 53 health checks are:

- Health checks that monitor an endpoint: You can configure a health check that monitors an endpoint that you specify either by IP address or by the domain name
- Health checks that monitor other health checks (calculated health checks): You can create a health check that monitors whether Route 53 considers other health checks healthy or unhealthy
- Health checks that monitor CloudWatch Alarms: You can create CloudWatch alarms that monitor the status of CloudWatch metrics, such as the number of throttled read events for an Amazon DynamoDB database or the number of Elastic Load Balancing hosts that are considered healthy

227- Which of the following statements on the egress-only internet gateway is incorrect?

    A. An egress-only internet gateway is stateful

    B. You can associate a security group with an egress-only internet gateway

    C. You can use a network ACL to control the traffic to and from the subnet for which the egress-only internet gateway routes traffic

    D. An egress-only internet gateway is for use with IPv6 traffic only

Answer: **B**

Explanation: An egress-only internet gateway is stateful. It forwards the traffic from the instance in the subnet to the internet or other AWS service and then sends reply to the instance. A security group cannot be associated with an internet gateway for egress only. You can use security groups to monitor traffic to and from those instances for your instance in your private subnet. The Network ACL may be used to regulate traffic from and to the subnet for which traffic is carried out via the internet gateway.

228- Which one of the following option can be used as a mean of classifying and managing network traffic and of providing Quality of Service (QoS) in modern layer 3 IP network?

    A. BFD
    B. BGP
    C. DSCP
    D. MEP

Answer: **C**

Explanation: Differentiated Service Code Point (DSCP) is used as a means of classification and network traffic management and service quality (QoS) delivery within modern IP Layer 3 networks. For packet classification, the IP field uses the 6-bit Differentiated Services (DS) field. Service Differentiation (Diffserv) is an architecture that sets out a straightforward scalable process to classify network traffic and manage service quality (QoS) in contemporary IP networks.

229- Which services can be used to monitor changes in your infrastructure?

    A. AWS CloudTrail
    B. AWS CloudWatch
    C. AWS CloudWatch logs
    D. AWS Config

Answer: **D**

Explanation: AWS Config affords an in-depth view of the configuration of AWS sources on your AWS account. This includes how the assets are related to one another and how they are configured within the past.

230- How many network interfaces do an AWS workspace have?

    A. 1
    B. 2
    C. 3
    D. 4

Answer: **B**

Explanation: The primary network interface provides connectivity to the resource within your VPC as well as the internet and is used to join the Workspace to the directory. The network management interface is connected to the Amazon WorkSpaces secure network of management. It is used for interactive streaming of the WorkSpaces desktop to Amazon WorkSpaces customers and for managing WorkSpaces from Amazon.

231- You have Linux EC2 instances hosted in AWS, and you want to create the script that can use the trace path command. Which of the following protocol can be open up in the security groups?

    A. TCP
    B. UDP
    C. ICMP
    D. SSL

Answer: **B**

Explanation: Trace path works on the UDP protocol. So, you need to open the UDP protocol in security group.

232- If the EC2 Linux instance supports enhanced networking, which of the following protocol can be used to check whether enhanced networking is enabled or not?

    A. Networkping
    B. Ethtool
    C. Awsnetwork
    D. Tracert

Answer: **B**

Explanation: Ethtool is the utility used for Linux kernel-based operating system for displaying and modifying some parameters of Network Interface Controllers (NICs) and other device drivers.

233- A website is hosted on 10 EC2 instances in 5 regions across the globe having two instances per region. How can you configure the site with minimum downtime to maintain the availability, if one of the five regions were to lose network connectivity for an extended period? Select the best choice from the given options.

A. Establish VPN connections between the instances in each region. Rely on BGP to failover in the case of region-wide connectivity failure for an extended period

B. Create a Route 53 latency-based routing record set that resolves to an Elastic Load Balancer in each region and has the evaluate target health flag set to true

C. Create a Route 53 latency-based routing record set that resolves to an Elastic Load Balancer in each region. Set an appropriate health check on each ELB

D. Create an Elastic Load Balancer to place in front of the EC2 instances. Set an appropriate health check on each ELB

Answer: **B**

Explanation: If your application is hosted in multiple AWS regions, you could enhance overall performance in your users by serving their requests from the AWS location that offers the best latency. For this, use Route 53 latency based routing. The Evaluate Target Health Check ensures the availability. If anyone of the region fails, evaluate target sets to true. Then the request will be sent to another region.

234- A person created a VPC having public and private subnets. That VPC has CIDR 20.0.0.0/16. The private subnet makes use of CIDR 20.0.1.0/24, and the public subnet makes use of CIDR 20.0.0.0/24. The user plans to host the web server in the public subnet (port 80) and a DB subnet with the private subnet (port 3306). The user is configuring the security group of the NAT instance. Which of the following mentioned entries are not required for the NAT security group?

A. For inbound, allow source: 20.0.1.0/24 on port 80

B. For outbound, allow destination: 0.0.0.0/0 on port 80

C. For inbound, allow source: 20.0.0.0/24 on port 80

D. For outbound, allow destination: 0.0.0.0/0on port 443

Answer: **C**

Explanation: You can use a Network Address Translation (NAT) instance in a public subnet for your VPC to enable instances inside the private subnet to provoke outbound IPv4 visitors to the internet or other AWS services, but prevent it from receiving inbound traffic initiated by using someone at the NAT.

235- Which of the following is not the part of charges that can be acquired when using AWS CloudFront?

    A. Data Transfer In
    B. Data Transfer Out
    C. HTTP/HTTPS Requests
    D. Invalidation Requests

Answer: **A**

Explanation: AWS CloudFront charges are based on the actual usage of the services in four areas. Data Transfer Out, HTTP/HTTPS request, invalidation requests and dedicated IP custom SSL certificates that are associated with the CloudFront distribution.

236- You need to create a subnet in VPC that supports 19 hosts, and you need to be accurate. What is the correct CIDR that should be used?

    A. /27
    B. /24
    C. /28
    D. /25

Answer: **A**

Explanation: To be sure, each load balancer's subnet has a CIDR block with at least /27 bitmask (e.g.,10.0.0/27) and at least 8 free IPs, so that the Load Balancer can be properly scaled. These IP addresses are used by your load balancer to create links to the instances. As five IPs are reserved by AWS, eight need to be free so you have 19 host IPs available.

237-   What is the recommendation for the subnet required, when working with AWS workspace?

   A. Having one private and one public subnet
   B. Having two private and one public subnet
   C. Having one private and two public subnets
   D. Having two private and two public subnets

Answer: **B**

Explanation: Amazon Workspaces launch your Workspaces in a Virtual Private Cloud (VPC). If you use AWS Directory Service to create an AWS Managed Microsoft or a Simple AD, we recommend that you configure the VPC with one public subnet and two private subnets. Configure your directory to launch your Workspaces in the private subnets.

238-   Which service can be used to monitor your account activity in AWS?

   A. AWS CloudTrail
   B. AWS CloudWatch
   C. AWS CloudWatch logs
   D. Account Reports

Answer: **A**

Explanation: AWS CloudTrail is a provider that permits governance, compliance, operational auditing, and risk auditing of your AWS account. With CloudTrail, you may log, continuously reveal, and keep account interest associated with movements across your AWS infrastructure. CloudTrail gives an event record of your AWS account activity, consisting of actions taken via the AWS Management Console, AWS SDKs, command line tools, and different AWS offerings. This occasion history simplifies protection analysis, aid change monitoring, and troubleshooting.

239-   A company has 50 employees, and wants to use a directory service in AWS. Which one of the following is best suited?

   A. Simple AD
   B. AD Connector
   C. Microsoft AD hosted on an EC2 instance
   D. Microsoft AD

Answer: A

Explanation: Since the footprint is small, Simple AD service would be sufficient. Simple AD service is the standalone managed directory that is powered by the Samba 4 Active Directory Compatible server. It is available in two sizes:

- Small (Support up to 500 Users)
- Large (Support up to 5000 users)

240-   Which of the following statements on VPC Flow logs is incorrect?

    A. After you have created a flow log, you cannot change its configuration

    B. You can create a flow log for a VPC, a subnet, or a network interface

    C. Flow Log data is published to a log group in CloudWatch Log

    D. The log data is captured in real time

Answer: D

Explanation: Flow Log record represents the network flow. Each record captures the network flow for specific five tuples, for a specific capture window. 5-tuple is the set of 5 different values that specifies the source, destination, and protocol for an IP flow. The capture window is the duration of time in which the Flow Logs aggregate the data before publishing the Flow Log records. It takes around 10-15 minutes to capture the window. Flow Logs do not capture real-time log streams for your network interfaces.

241-   An application is built with AWS SDK. This application interacts with the AWS S3 service. This application is going to be deployed in a private subnet. Which of the following must be done to make sure that the application interacts with AWS S3 service?

    A. Make the subnet as a public subnet

    B. Attach an internet gateway to the VPC

    C. Create a VPC S3 endpoint

    D. Attach a Virtual Private Gateway to the VPC

Answer: C

Explanation: A VPC endpoint permits you to privately join your VPC to supported AWS offerings and VPC endpoint offerings powered using the non-public link without requiring an internet gateway, NAT tool, VPN connection, or AWS Direct connect connection. Instances to

your VPC do not require public IP addresses to communicate with assets inside the service. Site visitors between your VPC and the other provider do not go away from the Amazon network.

242-   When it comes to an Elastic Network Interface, which of the following statement is incorrect?

A. You can attach a network interface to an instance when it is running
B. You can detach the secondary network interface and attach it to another instance in the same subnet
C. You can detach the primary network interface and attach it to another instance in the same subnet
D. You have a secondary private IP for a Network Interface

Answer: **C**

Explanation: In an Elastic Network Interface:

- A network interface can be attached to an instance when it is running, when it is stopped, or when the instance is being launched
- You can detach the secondary network interface when the instance is running or stopped. However, you cannot detach the primary interface
- You could connect a network interface in a single subnet to an example in some other subnet within the identical VPC. Both, the network interface and the instance ought to live within the same AZ

243-   Which of the following features of S3 is available for the bucket owner that is not charged for the objects requested and downloaded from this bucket by a user?

A. Transfer Acceleration
B. Requester Pays
C. Billing Request
D. Reduced S3 Costs

Answer: **B**

Explanation: In general, bucket owners pay for all Amazon S3 Storage and records transfer expenses related to their bucket. A bucket owner, can configure a bucket to be a Requester Pays bucket. With Requester Pay buckets, the requester in preference to the bucket owner will pay

the cost of the request and the information downloaded from the bucket. The bucket proprietor usually pays the value of storing data.

244- You wanted to host both, a private and public hosted zone for the same domain name in Route 53. How can this be achieved?

    A. This is impossible in Route 53
    B. By creating different resources records in the same hosted zone
    C. By configuring split-view DNS in Route 53
    D. By creating one hosted zone with both the private and public option

Answer: **C**

Explanation: You can use Amazon Route 53 to configure split-view DNS, also known as split-horizon DNS. If you want to maintain the internal and external version of the same application and website, you can configure the public and private hosted zones to return different internal and external IP addresses for the same domain name.

245- Which of the following CIDR notation is assigned to a subnet that holds the IPv6 address?

    A. /32
    B. /48
    C. /56
    D. /64

Answer: **D**

Explanation: For IPV6, the subnet mask is fixed to be a /64. Only one IPV6 CIDR block can be allocated to a subnet.

246- An AWS infrastructure currently has 4 VPCs. Your company has established AWS Direct Connect connection from on-premises to the AWS infrastructure. How many private interfaces can you configure?

    A. None. You can set the resources in the VPC in the normal way
    B. One. One virtual interface is enough for accessing the VPCs
    C. Four. One virtual interface for each VPC
    D. Eight. Two virtual interfaces (one for incoming and one for outgoing) for each VPC

Answer: **C**

Explanation: For private virtual interface, you need one private virtual interface for each VPC to connect from the AWS Direct Connect Connection.

247- Which steps should be taken in implementation to ensure the high availability of the NAT instance in AWS? (Choose 2)

    A. Deploy 2 NAT instances

    B. Place the NAT instances behind an ELB

    C. Create a script to monitor the primary NAT instance

    D. Deploy one or more NAT instance and ensure that, this second instance will take over when the primary NAT instance fails

Answer: **C & D**

Explanation: In Amazon Virtual Private Cloud (VPC), you can use private subnets for instances that you do not want to be directly addressable from the internet. Instances in a private subnet can access the internet without exposing their private IP addresses by routing their traffic through a Network Address Translation (NAT) instance in a public subnet. A NAT instance, however, can introduce a single point of failure to your VPC's outbound traffic. So for high availability, you can create one or more NAT instances and create a script that monitors primary NAT and failover to secondary NAT instance on the failure of primary NAT instance.

248- Which of the following service helps you to get a Classic Load Balancer API calls?

    A. CloudTrail

    B. CloudWatch

    C. CloudWatch Logs

    D. AWS Config

Answer: **A**

Explanation: To acquire a history of Classic Load Balancer API calls made for your account, activate the CloudTrail inside the AWS Management Console.

249- A user created a VPC with the general public subnet. The user has terminated all the instances that are the part of this subnet. Which statement is accurately consistent with the mentioned scenario?

    A. The user cannot delete the VPC since the subnet is not deleted
    B. All network interface attached with the instances will be deleted
    C. When the user launches a new instance, it cannot use the same subnet
    D. The subnet to which the instances were launched with will be deleted

Answer: **B**

Explanation: When you terminate an instance, the Elastic Network Interface will also be deleted.

250- A user has configured an ELB to distribute the traffic among multiple instances, but user instances are facing some issues due to backend servers. Which of the following mentioned CloudWatch metrics help the user to understand the issue with these instances?

    A. HTTPCode_Backend_3XX
    B. HTTPCode_Backend_4XX
    C. HTTPCode_Backend_2XX
    D. HTTPCode_Backend_5XX

Answer: **D**

Explanation: HTTPCode_Backend_5XX

Motive: A server blunders response sent from the registered times.

Solution: View the access logs or the mistake logs of your instances to decide the motive. Send requests immediately to the instance (bypass the load balancer) to view the responses.

251- Once you have created an AWS Direct Connect connection, how can you start working with connecting to resources in your VPC and other public resources? (Choose 2)

    A. By creating a VPC Peering connection
    B. By creating a Private Virtual Interface
    C. By creating a Private link connection
    D. By creating a Public Virtual Interface

Answer: **B & D**

Explanation: After you have placed an order for an AWS Direct Connect Connection, you should create a virtual interface before the usage of it. You may create a private virtual interface to hook up with your VPC, or you may create a virtual public interface to connect with AWS services that are not present in VPC.

252-   What is the bandwidth limit of the internet gateway provided by AWS?

    A. 50Mbps
    B. 100Mbps
    C. 200Mbps
    D. There is no limit

Answer: **D**
Explanation: Internet gateway is horizontally scaled, redundant and highly available. It imposes no bandwidth constraints.

253-   You are currently using Route 53 for DNS routing. Your application is hosted on Ec2 instances across multiple regions to ensure that the user across the world gets the best experience. Which of the following helps in this scenario?

    A. Configuring Geolocation routing policies in Route 53
    B. Configuring latency-based routing policies in Route 53
    C. Configuring weighted-based routing policies in Route 53
    D. Configuring failover-based routing policies in Route 53

Answer: **B**
Explanation: In case your application is hosted in multiple Amazon EC2 regions, you can enhance performance to your person by serving the request from the Amazon EC2 vicinity that provides the lowest latency. For this, you can configure latency-based routing.

254-   When you want to create an AWS Direct Connect connection in the AWS Console, which two of the following are required? (Choose 2)

    A. AWS Direct Connect Location
    B. The Virtual Private Gateway
    C. The Customer Gateway

D. The Port Speed

Answer: **A & D**

Explanation: Working with an accomplice in the AWS Partner Network (APN) will help you establish community circuits among an AWS Direct connect location and your data center, office, or colocation environment.

AWS Direct connect supports those port speeds over Single Mode Fiber: 1 Gbps: 1000BASE-LX (1310nm) and 10 Gbps: 10GBASE-LR (1310nm).

255-   You configured a web server listening on port 80 on an EC2 instance. You are trying to reach the home page of the web server but are unable to do so. You have checked that the internet gateway is attached to VPC and route tables have been modified accordingly. You have also attached an Elastic IP address to the EC2 instance. What can be done to solve this issue?

   A. Check the outbound security group rules; this could be denying the traffic on port 80
   B. Check the inbound rules for the NACL; this could be denying the traffic
   C. You need to have a public IP defined for the EC2 instance since the Elastic IP will not work
   D. Change the internet gateway as there could be an issue with the internet gateway

Answer: **B**

Explanation: If you have DENY rule for the port traffic that is lower in precedence for the NACL, this could also be a reason as to why the traffic is getting blocked. Allow inbound traffic because network ACLs are stateless, you must create inbound and outbound rules.

256-   You have acquired a new contract from a client to move all the existing infrastructure onto AWS. You noticed that some of the applications are using multicast and these applications need to keep running when migrated to AWS. You noticed that multicast is not available on AWS as you cannot manage multiple subnets on a single interface on AWS and a subnet can only belong to one AZ. Which of the following will enable you to deploy legacy applications on AWS that require multicast?

   A. Provide Elastic Network Interfaces between the subnets
   B. Create a virtual overlay network that runs on the OS-level of the instance
   C. Create all the subnets on a different VPC and use VPC peering between them

D. All of the answers listed will help in deploying applications that require multicast on AWS

Answer: **B**

Explanation: The recommended solution is to use Virtual Overlay Network. Overlay multicast is a way of constructing IP level multicast throughout a network fabric supporting unicast IP routing, which includes Amazon Virtual Private Cloud (Amazon VPC). We focus on an overlay multicast topology implemented using built-in features of Linux. This enables us to deploy multicast-aware applications in Amazon VPC.

257-   You have migrated an application from customer on-premises data center to AWS cloud. You are using ELB to serve traffic to the legacy application. The ELB is also using HTTP port 80 as the health check ping port. The application responds by returning a text file on port 80 when you check the IP address directly. However, the instance is registering as unhealthy while the appropriate amount of time has passed for the health check to register as healthy. How might be the issue resolved?

  A. By changing the ELB listener port from ping port 80 to HTTPS port 80, for instance to register as healthy

  B. By changing the ELB listener port from HTTP port 80 to TCP port 80, for instance to register as healthy

  C. By changing the ELB listener port from HTTP port 80 to HTTPS port 80, for instance to register as healthy

  D. By changing the ELB listener port from HTTP port 80 to TCP port 443, for instance to register as healthy

Answer: **B**

Explanation: Since the application is custom application and not a standard HTTP application, you need to have the TCP port open. Elastic Load Balancing supports HTTP, HTTPS, TCP, and SSL. You must configure one or more listeners for your Classic Load Balancer before you begin using Elastic Load Balancing. A listener is a connection request monitoring method. It is configured with a protocol and port to be used on the front-end (load balancer customer) links, a protocol and the back-end port.

258-   Which of the following are pre-requisites to enable cross-region replication between S3 buckets? (Choose 2)

A. The source and destination buckets must have versioning enabled

B. The source and destination buckets must have MFA enabled

C. The source and destination buckets must be in different AWS regions

D. The source and destination buckets must be in different AWS AZs

Answer: **A & C**

Explanation: Requirements for cross-region replication:

- The source and destination buckets must have versioning enabled
- The source and destination buckets must be in different AWS regions

259- Which factors would determine the EC2 Network performance? (Choose 3)

A. The attached EBS volume

B. EC2 instance size

C. Location of the EC2 instance

D. EC2 instance maximum transmission out

Answer: **B, C, & D**

Explanation: The following factors determine the network performance:

- The instance sizes. The larger instance provides better performance
- EC2 instance Maximum Transmission Unit (MTU)
- Location of the EC2 instance

A. A company has just set up a new document server on its AWS VPC, and it has four clients for which it wants to give access to. These clients also have VPC on AWS, and through this VPC, they are given access to the document server. Additionally, no client has the access to any other client's VPC. How can the client VPCs and the document server be connected?Setup a VPC peering between your company's VPC and each of the client's VPC

B. Setup VPC peering between your company's VPC and each of the client's VPC, but block the IPs from CIDR of the clients VPC to deny them access to each other

C. Setup VPC peering between your company's VPC and each of the client VPCs. Each client should have VPC peering set up between each other to speed up access time

D. Set up all the VPCs with the same CIDR but have your company's VPC as a centralized VPC

Answer: A

Explanation: A VPC peering connection is a networking connection among two VPCs, which allows you to direct traffic among them privately. Instances in both VPCs can communicate with each other and to every resource in peered VPCs as though they are within the equal community. You could create a VPC peering connection among your VPCs, with a VPC in any other AWS account, or with a VPC in a distinctive AWS place.

260- By which of the following ways does AWS Direct Connect connection set up? (Choose 3)

    A. At an AWS Direct Connect location

    B. Via an AWS Partner Network

    C. Via an existing VPN connection

    D. Through a hosted connection provided by a member of the APN

Answer: A, B, & D

Explanation:

You can set up AWS Direct Connection by the following method:

- At an AWS Direct Connect location
- Through the member of APN and network carrier
- Through a hosted connection provided by the member of APN

261- When AWS claims that VPC can work in dual-stack mode, what does it mean?

    A. The VPC has operated on both the TCP and UDP protocol at the same time

    B. The VPC can have an internet gateway and customer gateway attached at the same time

    C. The VPC can operate in both IPv4 and IPv6

    D. The VPC can have an internet gateway and Virtual Private Gateway attached at the same time

Answer: C

Explanation: The VPC can operate in dual-stack mode, your resources can communicate over IPV4 and IPv6 or both. IPV4 and IPV6 communication are independent of each other.

262- When using AWS Direct Connect, what is the pricing of inbound traffic?

    A. $0.02 per GB in all locations
    B. It depends on the region for the Direct Connect connection
    C. It depends on the AZ for the Direct Connect connection
    D. $0.00 per GB in all locations

Answer: **D**

Explanation: Data transfer In charge is 0.00$ per GB in all locations.

263- Which of the following cannot be used to enable the proxy control on Classic Load Balancer?

    A. The AWS API
    B. A script which uses the AWS CLI
    C. The AWS CLI
    D. The AWS Management Console

Answer: **D**

Explanation: The AWS Management Console does not support the enabling proxy protocol.

264- You currently have a set of EC2 instances in a private subnet that communicates to the internet through the NAT instances. You plan to use the NAT gateway by replacing the NAT instances. Which of the following will be noted during the transition?

    A. You can safely do the transition since during the transition; the existing connections will be moved from the NAT instance to the gateway
    B. The existing connections to the NAT instance will go through a connection draining period. Therefore, there will be no disruptions to the existing service
    C. There will be a slight disruption that would need to be accounted for because the current connections to the NAT instance will be dropped
    D. It is not possible to replace a NAT gateway with a NAT instance

Answer: **C**

Explanation: If you change the routing from NAT gateway to NAT instance, or if you disassociate the Elastic IP from NAT instance. Current connection will be dropped and re-established. Make sure that you do not have any critical task running.

265-   A set of EC2 instances is a part of the public subnet in a VPC, and you have to ensure that the administrator can only SSH from the workstation with the IP 59.12.10.10. Which of the following CIDR blocks must be added to the inbound rules for the security groups to fulfill the requirement?

   A. 59.12.10.10/28
   B. 59.12.10.10/16
   C. 59.12.10.10/32
   D. 59.12.10.10/24

Answer: **C**
Explanation: The /32 address must be specified as a single IP address and added to the security group accordingly.

266-   You plan to use the CIDR block of 10.0.1.0/27 to design the subnet in AWS. How many subnets are possible with this CIDR block?

   A. 1*27
   B. 2*28
   C. 2*32
   D. 4*16

Answer: **B**
Explanation: In AWS, the VPC is limited up to /28 CIDR range. So, the maximum number of subnets is 2.

267-   A VPN is set up between AWS and on-premises network. An EC2 instance is launched in the VPC to check the connections between them using the ping command. Which of the given options are applicable to ensure that the test would be performed according to the requirement? (Choose 3)

   A. Ensure the security groups allow Inbound ICMP traffic
   B. Ensure the security groups allow Outbound ICMP traffic
   C. Ensure the network groups allow Inbound ICMP traffic

D. Ensure the network groups allow Outbound ICMP traffic

Answer: **A, C, & D**

Explanation: You have created the VPN connection and configured the customer gateway. You can launch the instance and check the connection by using the ping command. You need an AMI that responds to a ping request, and you need to make sure that your instance's security group is configured to enable inbound ICMP. Remember the security groups are stateful so you do not need to make sure that outbound traffic is allowed. For network group, you need to allow both inbound and outbound ICMP traffic as it is stateless.

268-   When creating a VPN connection in AWS, which of the following is required? (Choose 2)

    A. Customer gateway
    B. Internet gateway
    C. Virtual Private gateway
    D. BGP

Answer: **A & C**

Explanation: A Virtual Private Gateway is the VPN connector on the AWS factor of the VPN connection. You should create a virtual gateway and set it as non-public, then attach it to the VPC from which you want to create the VPN connection. A customer gateway is a tool or software in your side of the VPN connection.

269-   You have created a custom VPC and a subnet. You have launched the EC2 instance in that instance, but you have noticed that a public IP address is not assigned to the EC2 instance. What steps should be taken to make sure that EC2 instance will get the public IP address? (Choose 2)

    A. Ensure an internet gateway is attached to the VPC
    B. Ensure the auto-assign attribute for the subnet is marked as 'yes'
    C. Ensure that whether the EC2 instance is launched or not
    D. Ensure that when the wizard is used during the launch time of the Ec2 instance, the setting is marked as enabled for public IP for the EC2 instance

Answer: **B & D**

Explanation: By default, non-default subnets have the IPv4 public addressing attribute set to false, and default subnets have this attribute set to true. An exception is a non-default subnet

created by the Amazon EC2 launch instance wizard; the wizard sets the attribute to true. You can modify this attribute using the Amazon VPC console.

270-   Which of the techniques can be used to minimize the surface of DDoS attacks on AWS infrastructure? (Choose 3)

    A. Use SQS queues to absorb the requests from the attack
    B. Deploy a Load Balancer in front of your computational resource
    C. Deploy a CloudFront distribution in front of your computational resource
    D. Use NACL's to control the flow of traffic

Answer: **B, C, & D**

Explanation: One of the first techniques to mitigate DDoS attacks is to minimize the surface area that can be attacked thereby limiting the options for attackers and allowing you to build protections in a single place. We want to ensure that we do not expose our application or resources to ports, protocols or applications from where they do not expect any communication. Thus, minimizing the possible points of attack and letting us concentrate our mitigation efforts. In some cases, you can do this by placing your computation resources behind Content Distribution Networks (CDNs) or Load Balancers and restricting direct internet traffic to certain parts of your infrastructure like your database servers. In other cases, the traffic reaches your applications via firewalls or the Access Control Lists (ACLs).

271-   To do a deep dive into the packets sent across EC2 instances, which services are used?

    A. Cloud Watch
    B. Cloud Trail
    C. Flow Logs
    D. None of the above

Answer: **D**

Explanation: The three given services do not provide deep dive, you need to use a custom software for this purpose.

272- Which of the following features of S3 would allow the large transfer of files over a long distance?

    A. Requester Pays
    B. Transfer Acceleration
    C. Fast Transfer
    D. Multi-part File Upload

Answer: **B**

Explanation: Amazon S3 Transfer Acceleration enables speedy, easy, and relaxed transfers of files over lengthy distances among your consumer and an S3 bucket. Transfer Acceleration takes advantage of Amazon CloudFront's globally distributed edge location. As the statistics arrive at an edge location, data is routed to Amazon S3 over an optimized network route.

273- When you launch an instance with the default settings in default VPC, which one the following will automatically be generated for that instance? (Choose 3)

    A. Private IP address
    B. Elastic IP address
    C. Private DNS hostname
    D. Public DNS hostname

Answer: **A, C, & D**

Explanation: When an instance is launched in the default VPC, AWS provides the public and private DNS hostnames that correspond to the public and private IPv4 addresses for the instance.

274- Which of the following are the valid properties of the placement group? (Choose 3)

    A. A cluster placement group can span across multiple AZs
    B. Placement groups cannot be merged
    C. An instance can be launched in one placement group at a time; it cannot span multiple placement groups
    D. You cannot move an existing instance into a placement group
    E. If you want to delete a placement group, you need to terminate or move all instances from it

Answer: **B, C, & E**

Explanation: The limitations on placement groups are:

- A placement group cannot span across multiple AZs
- You cannot merge placement groups
- A placement group can span over peered VPCs

275- You have created 5 VPCs in Ireland region and attached them with an internet gateway. When you try to create another internet gateway, you are unable to do so. What might be the reason?

   A. You need to create a VPC before you create an internet gateway
   B. You need to ensure the VPC is public before you can create an internet gateway
   C. You have crossed the threshold of 4 internet gateways
   D. You have crossed the threshold of 5 internet gateways

Answer: **D**

Explanation: The limit is directly co-related with the limits on VPC per region. But you cannot increase this limit individually. The only way to increase this limit is to increase the limits on VPCs per regions. Only one gateway is attached to one VPC at a time.

276- Which of the following options allow private EC2 instances in your VPC to work with the AWS resources without the need of an internet gateway, NAT device, public IP address, or VPN connection?

   A. Public Link
   B. VPC Link
   C. Private Link
   D. AWS Link

Answer: **C**

Explanation: AWS Private Link is a highly available, scalable technology that enables you to connect your VPC to supported AWS services privately, services hosted by other AWS accounts (VPC endpoint services), and supported AWS Marketplace partner services. You do not require an internet gateway, NAT device, public IP address, AWS Direct Connect connection, or AWS Site-to-Site VPN connection to communicate with the service. Traffic between your VPC and the service does not leave the Amazon network.

277-   Which of the following is used to verify whether your AWS infrastructure is under DDoS attack or not? (Choose 2)

    A. EC2 CPU Utilization
    B. ELB Surge Queue Length
    C. Healthy Host Count
    D. Unhealthy Host Count

Answer: **A & B**

Explanation:

The CPU Utilization of the backend instances can indicate that backend instances are under tremendous load. Surge queue length is defined by the number of requests that are queued by the ELB. These processes are queued when the back-end system is unable to process the incoming request as fast as requests are being received.

278-   If a VPN connection exists between an on-premises facility and AWS, and workspaces are also being used, then what is the minimum amount of MTU that is supported by the connection?

    A. 500
    B. 900
    C. 1200
    D. 1500

Answer: **C**

Explanation: If users access their Workspaces through VPN, the connection must support the Maximum Transmission Unit (MTU) of at least 1200 bytes.

279-   You have just set up a Classic Load Balancer with EC2 instances distributed over two subnets. The first subnet has one instance while the second subnet contains three instances. You have found that the load is high on the first subnet, which contains only one instance. Which of the following settings can be implemented to Load Balancer for even distribution of the traffic across the instances?

    A. Configure connection draining
    B. Configure sticky sessions

C. Configure proxy protocols

D. Configure cross-zone load balancing

Answer: D

Explanation: With cross-zone load balancing, each load balancer node for your Classic Load Balancer distributes requests evenly across the registered instances in all enabled Availability Zones. If cross-zone load balancing is disabled, each load balancer node distributes requests evenly across the registered instances in its Availability Zone only.

280- A VPC currently has two subnets in an AWS. The VPC contains the CIDR block of 10.0.0.0/16, and the subnets have a CIDR block of 10.0.1.0/24 and 10.0.2.0/24 respectively. You decide to create a custom route table on each subnet. When you initially create a custom route table, which of the following routes are present by default in the route table?

A. A route for 10.0.0.0/16 as the destination

B. A route for 10.0.1.0/24 as the destination

C. A route for 10.0.2.0/24 as the destination

D. There will be no default route in the route table

Answer: A

Explanation: By default, when a new route table is created, it will have a default route for the CIDR block of the VPC. Every route table contains a local route to communicate to others in VPC over IPV4.

281- Which of the following is not a recommended private IP range to be used while defining the internal VPCs?

A. 10.0.0.0 – 10.255.255.255

B. 20.0.0.0 – 20.255.255.255

C. 172.16.0.0 – 172.31.255.255

D. 192.168.0.0 – 192.168.255.255

Answer: B

Explanation: When you create a VPC, we recommend that you specify a CIDR block (of /16 or smaller) from the private IPv4 address ranges as specified in RFC 1918:

- 10.0.0.0 - 10.255.255.255 (10/8 prefix)
- 172.16.0.0 - 172.31.255.255 (172.16/12 prefix)
- 192.168.0.0 - 192.168.255.255 (192.168/16 prefix)

282-   A company plans to use AWS Classic Load Balancer in AWS. You are preparing the subnet which can be used in the Load Balancer. Which of the following bit mask is required for the subnet to be used with the Load Balancer?

     A. /30
     B. /29
     C. /28
     D. /27

Answer: **D**

Explanation: To make sure that the load balancer is running properly, confirm that every subnet for your load balancer has a CIDR block with at least /27 masks and has as a minimum of eight free IP addresses. Your load balancer uses those IP addresses to keep the connection with the instances.

283-   Which of the following type of protocols is BGP classified as?

     A. Link State
     B. Distance Vector
     C. Path Vector
     D. Link Vector

Answer: **C**

Explanation: BGP is the standardized exterior routing protocol that is used to exchange routing and reachability information among AS on the internet. This vector is often classified as a path vector protocol.

284-   Which of the following is not an application implementation for establishing a hybrid network between on-premises and AWS?

     A. AWS Direct Connect
     B. VPC Peering
     C. Hardware VPN
     D. Software VPN

Answer: B

Explanation: VPC Peering is used for peering purpose, and not for creating a hybrid solution.

285- You have an application that is hosted on ELB with EC2 instances running in AWS. Route 53 is working as the DNS service. You plan to deploy a new version of the application, which will have the new ELB with EC2 instances but you want this transition to be phased out so that a number of users can get access to the new application. Once the application is confirmed as working, the entire user base can be switched over it. How can you configure Route 53?

    A. Configure Route 53 with the weighted routing policy
    B. Configure Route 53 with the failover routing policy
    C. Configure Route 53 with the latency routing policy
    D. Configure Route 53 with the simple routing policy

Answer: **A**

Explanation: Weighted routing makes you associate multiple resources with the single domain name or subdomain name and check how much traffic is routed to each resource. This can be useful for the variety of purposes that includes testing load balancing and testing a new version of the software.

286- You have three EC2 instances with public IP addresses that are mapped to DNS hostnames in Route 53. The Administrator advises you that this may not be the ideal setup and DNS name could point to invalid IP addresses in future. Select the best solution for this problem? (Choose 2)

    A. Map the DNS names to the private IP addresses
    B. Create Elastic IPs and assign them to the EC2 instances
    C. Map the DNS names to the Elastic IPs
    D. Ensure the instances receive private IP addresses

Answer: **B & C**

Explanation: When the instances stop and start, the public IP assigned to the instance changes, and this results in a broken DNS link. The ideal scenario is to have Elastic IP addresses and map them to the DNS hostnames.

287- You have nine EC2 instances running in a Placement Group. All of these instances were initially launched at the same time and they performed as expected. You decided to add two more instances to the group, but when you attempt to do this, you receive a "capacity error". What can be done to fix this issue?

    A. Make a new placement group and launch the new instances in the new group. Make sure the placement groups are in the same subnet

    B. Stop and restart the instances in the placement group and then try the launch again

    C. Request a capacity increase from AWS as you are initially limited to 10 instances per placement group

    D. Make sure all the instances are of the same size and then try the launch again

Answer: **B**

Explanation: If you get an InsufficientInstanceCapacity error when you try to launch an instance or restart a stopped instance, it means that AWS does not currently have enough available On-Demand capacity to complete your request. To resolve this issue, you can do the following:

- Wait a couple of minutes then request again; the capability can change often
- Send a new request with a small amount of instances. For example, if you are requesting 15 instances for a single request, try making three requests for five instead of 15 requests for one instance
- Submit new request without defining an AZ
- Request for new instance with different instance type
- Stop and restart the instance in placement group and then try to launch again

288- You have an EC2 instance based on the Amazon Linux AMI. You have created a secondary network interface and attached it to the running instance. How can you ensure that the network interface is configured correctly?

    A. Go ahead and add the interfaces to the network interfaces location on the instance

    B. Use the AWS CLI to configure the network interface

    C. The Amazon based instances do not accept secondary interfaces

    D. This will be configured automatically

Answer: **D**

Explanation: Launching an Amazon Linux and Window Server instance with multiple network interfaces will automatically configure the interfaces, private IPV4 addresses and route table on the OS of the instance.

289- A VPC with CIDR 20.0.0.0/16 has been created by a user. In this VPC, the user has created a subnet. The user attempts to create a different subnet for CIDR 20.0.0.1/24 using the same VPC. In this scenario, what is going to happen?

    A. It is not possible to create a subnet with the same CIDR as the VPC
    B. The second subnet will be created
    C. The VPC will modify the first subnet to allow this IP range
    D. It will throw a CIDR overlap error

Answer: **D**
Explanation: Since the CIDR overlaps for the first and the second subnet, an overlap error will occur.

290- Your task is an outbound communication over IPv6 from instances in your VPC to the Internet. Choose the correct option from the following to fulfill your task.

    A. Customer Gateway
    B. Egress-only Internet Gateway
    C. Virtual Private Connection
    D. Virtual Private Gateway

Answer: **B**
Explanation: An egress-only internet gateway is a horizontal, redundant and highly available VPC element that enables IPv6 communication from the VPC instances to the internet and prevents the it from establishing an IPv6 connection with your instance.

291- Five VPCs are available in AWS. In two VPCs, there is a server for file sharing. This file sharing service should be available across all other VPCs. Select 2 options from the following to do this. The options form a part of the solution.

    A. Create a full mesh configuration of VPC Peering with the VPCs
    B. Modify the Route tables of each VPC with the peering configuration

    C. Modify the VPC configuration of each VPC with the peering configuration

    D. Create Instances with enhanced networking to share the files across other VPCs

Answer: **A & B**

Explanation: To create a file sharing server, you need to peer all VPCs because there are multiple VPCs that require access to the files; a mesh configuration is necessary. To create a communication between peered VPCs, route tables of all the peered VPCs must be modified with peering configuration.

292- When you set up a virtual interface with Direct Connect, which of the following is the wrong statement when it comes to the configuration of BGP via virtual interface?

    A. A BGP session needs to have a public or private ASN number on the customer side

    B. If a public ASN is being used, then it must be ensured that you own the ASN

    C. Autonomous System (AS) prepending can work even if you use a private ASN for a public virtual interface

    D. If a private ASN is used, it must be in the 64512 to 65535 range

Answer: **C**

Explanation: For the BGP session, a virtual interface must be fitted with an Autonomous System Number (ASN) in the public or private Border Gateway Protocol (BGP). You have to own it if you use a public ASN. It must be in the 64512 to 65535 range for private ASN applications. AS prepending will not work if a public virtual interface is used with a private ASN. The authentication key can be supplied with your own MD5 BGP, or Amazon can create it for you.

293- Identify the first and last addresses (network and broadcast) for 10.0.0.0/25.

    A. 10.0.0.0 and 10.0.0.128

    B. 10.0.0.1 and 10.0.0.255

    C. 10.0.0.0 and 10.0.0.127

    D. 10.0.0.0 and 10.0.0.255

Answer: **C**

Explanation: For /25, you have maximum 128 addresses in a subnet, so the broadcast address is 10.0.0.127, network address is 10.0.0.0, and available IP addresses for host is 10.0.0.1 to 10.0.0.126. You can determine this by using any CIDR calculator.

294- Under a DDoS attack, you have denied all TCP rule to your NACL, but traffic does not get blocked. What could be the reason behind this?

    A. The DDoS is not a TCP attack
    B. NACL cannot protect against DDoS attacks
    C. You configured the rule number to be too low
    D. You need to add a deny rule outbound to the NACL

Answer: **A**

Explanation: There are different types of DDoS attacks;

- Volume based (Includes UDP floods, ICMP floods, and other spoofed-packet floods)
- Protocols based (Includes SYN floods, fragmented packet attacks, Ping of Death, Smurf DDoS and more)
- Application layer based (Includes low-and-slow attacks, GET/POST floods, attacks that target Apache, Windows or OpenBSD vulnerabilities and more)

295- Your network uses servers and routers with jumbo frames. You try to access your AWS resources and face problems with the loss of packets. What can be considered from the following options to rectify the problem?

    A. Call AWS support
    B. Consider using Direct Connect
    C. Consider Lowering the MTU for your network
    D. Remove the "Do not Fragment" flag on the packets

Answer: **D**

Explanation: Excessive retransmission may cause IP fragmentation. If fragments encounter the loss of a packet and reliable protocols such as the TCP must retransmit all fragments to recover the loss of one fragment.

296- Which of the following options is ideally applicable if you want to have a cluster of EC2 Instances with low network latency between them?

    A. Launch all of the instances with Security Groups that allow all network traffic
    B. Launch all of the instances in a placement group
    C. Launch all of the instances with NACLs that allow all network traffic

D. Launch all of the Instances as t2.micro instances

Answer: **B**

Explanation: A logical grouping of instances within a single Availability Zone is known as Placement group. They are recommended for applications that benefit from low network latency, high network throughput, or both. Choose a type of instance to support enhanced networking to provide you with the lowest latency and the highest network per second packet performance for your placement group.

297- If you want to operate connections in a Link Aggregation Group, which of the following mode would you select?

    A. Passive/Active mode
    B. Passive/Passive mode
    C. Active/Active mode
    D. Active/Passive mode

Answer: **C**

Explanation: All LAGs have attributes determining a minimum number of LAG connections that must be operational for the LAG itself to be operational. This attribute is set to "0" by default in new LAGs. You can update your LAG to specify a different value, which means your entire LAG will be unworkable if the number of operating connections fall below the limit. This attribute can be used to prevent the remaining connections being overused.

All connections in a LAG operate in Active/Active mode.

298- You plan to move your current DNS service to AWS Route 53. What is the first thing you should do for this in Route 53?

    A. Create a hosted zone
    B. Create a new domain name
    C. Create a AAA record
    D. Create a CNAME record

Answer: **A**

Explanation: Creating a host zone is the first step in AWS for migrating the domain from existing DNS service to AWS. Hosted zone contains all the information about your domain.

299- An on-premises location of a company is currently connected to a VPC. This company wants a dedicated on-site network connection to the VPC. Choose the correct answer from the following options to fulfill the given requirement.

    A. Provision a VPN connection between the on-premises data center and the AWS region using the VPN section of a VPC

    B. Use a hardware VPN to connect both locations

    C. Use a software VPN to connect both locations

    D. Suggest provisioning a Direct Connect connection between the on-premises data center and the AWS region

Answer: **D**

Explanation: AWS Direct Connect makes it easy to connect your premises to AWS with the dedicated network. You can establish private connectivity between AWS or your data center, office or co-location environment through AWS Direct Connect, which can, in many cases, reduce your network costs, boost bandwidth transmission and provide more consistent network experiences than on the internet.

300- A company is setting an Active/Passive Direct Connect connection to AWS, which of the following options would assist them?

    A. Route Propagation

    B. AS_PATH Prepending

    C. Virtual Private Gateway

    D. VPC Peering

Answer: **B**

Explanation: Active/Passive (failover) has one connection for handling traffic, and the other is on standby. If the active link is unavailable, the passive connection routes all the traffic. For this to become a passive link, you have to prepend the AS path on one of your links.

301- Your business has an on-site data center. You want to create a VPN connection to AWS. A highly available connection is required. Choose two options that would form a solution for this scenario.

    A. Create 2 Virtual Private Gateways

B. Create a Virtual Private Gateway

C. Create 2 Customer Gateways

D. Create a Customer Gateway

Answer: **B & C**

Explanation: Two Customer Gateways (CGW) and one Virtual Gateway (VGW) combine to form a highly available architecture for VPN connection.

302-   Choose the supported protocol for AWS VPN connection.

A. DES

B. AES

C. OpenSSL

D. IPSec

Answer: **D**

Explanation: The link between your VPC and your own network is referred to as a VPN connection. AWS supports Internet Protocol Security (IPSec) VPN connections.

303-   If you want to use IPv6 address that would include all IP addresses, which one will you choose?

A. 0.0.0.0:/0

B. 0.0.0.0

C. ::/0

D. 0.0.0.0.0.0.0.0

Answer: **C**

Explanation: ::/0 refers to the default route address for IPv6 (corresponding to 0.0.0.0/0 in IPv4) covering all addresses (unicast, multicast and others).

304-   Select the ones that get charged when using AWS Direct Connect.

A. port-hours

B. Subnets in VPC

C. VPCs in the region

   D. Data transfer

Answer: **A & D**

Explanation: There are two separate charges for AWS Direct Connect; port hours and data transfer. The prices for each port type are per port hour and partially consumed port hours are counted as full hours. The transfer of data through AWS Direct Connect is charged within the same month of its use. You will only be charged for the data transferred out of that virtual interface at the relevant data transfer rates if you have a Hosted Virtual Interface. Port-hour fees are paid to the port account.

305-   A Direct Connect Connection is extended from the parent company to AWS VPC via host Virtual Interface. What are the charges the company has to pay?

   A. You are only responsible for the port hours of the Virtual Interface
   B. You are responsible for all data transfer out
   C. You are not charged anything
   D. You are responsible for all data transfer in

Answer: **B**

Explanation: In the same month in which usage takes place, data transfer via AWS Direct Connect shall be invoiced. If your virtual interface is hosting, you are charged at applicable data transfer rates only for the data transferred out from that virtual interface.

306-   The instances of your application server reside in your VPC's private subnet. These instances must have access to an internet Git repository. In the public subnet of your VPC, you create a NAT gateway. This gateway can access the Git repository, whereas private subnet instances are not able to do this. In the private subnet route table, you confirm that a default path points to the NAT gateway. The security group for instances in your app server allows all NAT gateway traffic.
   What would you do to make sure these instances can reach the server?

   A. Configure an outbound rule on the application server instance security group for the Git repository
   B. Assign public IP addresses to the instances and route 0.0.0.0/0 to the Internet gateway
   C. Configure an inbound rule on the application server instance security group for the Git repository

D. Configure inbound network Access Control Lists (network ACLs) to allow traffic from the Git repository to the public subnet

Answer: A

Explanation: The traffic leaves the Git repository instance; the security group must allow it to pass at this point. The route then directs the traffic to the NAT gateway (based on the IP).

Option B is wrong because it removes the subnet's private aspect and does not affect blocked traffic.

Option C is incorrect because an output security group rule is needed to allow outgoing traffic to the Git repository.

Option D is wrong because outgoing traffic does not reach the NAT gateway.

307- An AWS have a Classic Load Balancer where backend instances work on TCP protocol. You want the client's IP which hit the Load Balancer. Choose the appropriate option for this.

A. Configure connection draining
B. Configure sticky sessions
C. Configure Cross-Zone Load balancing
D. Use the Proxy Protocol Header

Answer: D

Explanation: You can identify a client's IP address when you have a load balancer using TCP for backend connections via the Proxy Protocol Header. Due to the interception of the load balancers traffic between clients and your instances, your instance access logs include the IP address of the load balancer instead of the of the client originating. To retrieve the IP address and port number of your client, the first line of the request can be retrieved.

308- Choose the option that cannot be used for VPC to VPC connectivity.

A. AWS VPN CloudHub
B. Software VPN
C. Hardware VPN
D. VPC Peering

Answer: A

Explanation: AWS VPN CloudHub is used to connect AWS VPC with on-site datacenters. For VPC to VPC connectivity you can use VPC peering, Software VPN, Hardware VPN and AWS Direct Connect.

309-   What is the best method to prevent a number of attacks from a set of defined IP ranges?

    A. Create web Security Group rules to block the attacking IP addresses over port 80

    B. Put the application on the private subnet

    C. Create an inbound NACL (Network Access Control List) associated with the web tier subnet with denying rules to block the attacking IP addresses

    D. Create a custom route table associated with the web tier and block the attacking IP addresses from the IGW (Internet GateWay)

Answer: **C**

Explanation: An ACL is an optional security layer for your VPC to act as a firewall in and out of one or more subnet traffic control. You may set up ACLs in order to add an additional layer of security to your VPC by blocking the attacking IPs.

310-   Select the AWS service that is best for working on its own to assist in mitigating a large scale global DDOS attack.

    A. AWS SQS

    B. AWS EC2

    C. AWS ELB

    D. AWS CloudFront

Answer: **D**

Explanation: Traffic across multiple Points-of-Presence (PoP) locations is distributed by Amazon CloudFront and filters requests to ensure that only valid HTTP(S) requests will be forwarded to backend hosts. CloudFront supports geo-restriction, also referred to as geo blocking. This can be useful for isolating attacks from a specific geographical location.

311-Your company assigned you a task to create a subnet that has the capacity to host 512 addresses. Which network masks would you use to ensure that you are as accurate as possible when hosting these IP addresses?

A. /23

B. /24

C. /22

D. /21

Answer: **C**

Explanation: If you have a /23 subnet mask, you will have exactly 512 hosts; five IPs are not available because they are reserved. So, you will end up with 507 hosts that do not meet the needs. Therefore, option C is correct.

You are not provided with and cannot assign the initial four IP addresses and the last IP address for each CIDR block subnet. For example, the following five IP addresses are reserved for a subnet with CIDR block 10.0.0.0/24:

10.0.0.0: Network address.

10.0.0.1: It is reserved by AWS for the VPC router.

10.0.0.2: It is reserved by AWS.

The IP address of the DNS server is always the base of the VPC network range plus two; however, we also reserve the base of each subnet range plus two. 10.0.0.3: Reserved by AWS for future use.

10.0.0.255: Network Broadcast address. AWS does not support broadcast in a VPC. Therefore, we reserve this address.

312-   Select the attribute that is not associated with Elastic Network Interface.

A. MAC Address

B. NACL

C. Source/Destination Check Flag

D. Security Groups

Answer: **B**

Explanation: Given below is the list of network interface attributes:

• A MAC addresses

• One public IPv4 address

• One Elastic IP address (IPv4) per private IPv4 address

• One or more secondary private IPv4 addresses

• A description

• One or more IPv6 addresses

• A source/destination check flag

- One or more security groups
- A primary private IPv4 address

313- What would be the default value of ASN assigned to the connection when you create a VPN in AWS using VPC wizard?

    A. 64000

    B. 65000

    C. 66000

    D. 67000

Answer: **B**

Explanation: If you do not have an existing ASN assigned to your network, you can use a private ASN. To set up a VPC by using VPC wizard, AWS automatically assigns ASN, i.e., 65000

314- A total of five VPCs in a region have been created. What could be the reason that you are unable to create the 6th VPC?

    A. The region does not support creating of VPCs

    B. There is already a VPC present with the same CIDR block range

    C. There is a limit of five VPCs per region. Submit a request to get the limit increased

    D. There is already a VPC with the same name defined

Answer: **C**

Explanation: By default, per region limit of VPC is 5. For changing that limit, you have to send a request.

315- As an AWS professional, you have to ensure uniform traffic to an application. The application has several web servers that host the application. Choose the suitable option that meets the requirements.

    A. Configure a CloudFront distribution and configure the origin to point to the private IP addresses of your Web servers. Configure a Route 53 CNAME record to your CloudFront distribution

    B. Configure ELB with an EIP. Place all your Web servers behind ELB Configure a Route 53 A record that points to the EIP

C. Configure a NAT instance in your VPC. Create a default route via the NAT instance and associate it with all subnets. Configure a DNS A record that points to the NAT instance public IP address

D. Place all your web servers behind ELB. Configure a Route 53 CNAME to point to the ELB DNS name

Answer: **D**

Explanation: You do not want to point CloudFront to private IP Addresses and also, a NAT instance is ideally used to route traffic from a private subnet to the internet via a public subnet. For the given scenario, you can use an ELB, assign the web servers and have a Route 53 entry to the ELB.

316- Choose 2 options that can be used with CloudFront to serve private content.

A. Use Signed Distributions
B. Use Signed Objects
C. Use Signed Cookies
D. Use Signed URLs

Answer: **C & D**

Explanation: CloudFront can be configured to require users to access your objects using signed URLs or cookies.

317- Your company wants to check the details of ENIs in a particular region, which of the following commands would you suggest to them?

A. describe-network-interfaces
B. get-network-interfaces
C. get-network-cards
D. describe-ENI

Answer: **A**

Explanation: "describe-network-interfaces" command can be used to obtain information about single or multiple network interfaces.

318- You have to create an AWS Cloud presence. The Cloud has been assigned the IP address range 11.11.253.0/24. Not considering the reserved IP addresses for subnets, choose the number of subnets and hosts available for this CIDR range.

    A. 128 maximum number of subnets and 254 number of hosts

    B. 256 maximum number of subnets and 254 number of hosts

    C. 256 maximum number of subnets and 256 number of hosts

    D. 256 maximum number of subnets and 128 number of hosts

Answer: **B**

Explanation: For maskbit /24, you have $2^{(32-24)} = 2^8 = 256$ number of subnets. From the 256, you have 1 broadcast and one network IP address therefore, you have 254 number of available host IPs.

319- In order to avoid SQL Injection attacks against the infrastructure in AWS, which of the given option is best?

    A. Create NACL rules for the subnet hosting the application

    B. Add a WAF tier by creating a new ELB and an Auto Scaling group of EC2 Instances running a host-based WAF. They would redirect Route 53 to resolve to the new WAF tier ELB. The WAF tier would pass the traffic to the current web tier. The web tier Security Groups would be updated to only allow traffic from the WAF tier Security Group

    C. Remove all but TLS 1 & 2 from the web tier ELB and enable Advanced Protocol Filtering. This will enable the ELB itself to perform WAF functionality

    D. Create a Direct Connect connection so that you have a dedicated connection line

Answer: **B**

Explanation: AWS WAF is a firewall for web applications that protect your web applications from common web exploits that may affect the availability of applications, compromise security or consume excessive resources. AWS WAF can be used to create custom rules that block common attack patterns such as SQL injection or cross-site scripting, and rules that are designed for your specific application. New rules can be deployed within minutes, letting you respond quickly to the changing traffic patterns.

320- Select the current limit for transferring data per distribution in CloudFront?

A. 500 Gbps
B. 200 Gbps
C. 100 Gbps
D. 40 Gbps

Answer: **D**

Explanation: AWS provides the general limit of 40 Gbps for data transfer rate per distribution in CloudFront.

321-   Choose the option which represents the number of public IP addresses that can be assigned to an Elastic Network Interface.

A. 0
B. 1
C. 2
D. 3

Answer: **B**

Explanation: Given below is the list of network interface attributes:

- A MAC addresses
- One public IPv4 address
- One Elastic IP address (IPv4) per private IPv4 address
- One or more secondary private IPv4 addresses
- A description
- One or more IPv6 addresses
- A source/destination check flag
- One or more security groups
- A primary private IPv4 address

322-   Select 3 port numbers that should be opened for the proper functioning of AWS workspaces.

A. Port 80
B. Port 443
C. Port 22
D. Port 53

Answer: A, B, & D

Explanation: Major ports that are necessary to be open for AWS WorkSpaces are as follows:

- Port 80 (UDP and TCP) - This port is used for initial connections to http://clients/amazonworkspaces.com, which then switch to HTTPS

- Port 443 (TCP) – This port is used for updating, registering, and authenticating client applications. The desktop client applications support the use of a proxy server for port 443 (HTTPS) traffic

- Port 53(UDP) - This port is used for accessing DNS servers

323- Your data center and VPC are connected via static VPN with 50 routes in the route table. What would you do to add more routes?

    A. Increase the number of route tables

    B. Increase the number of VPCs

    C. Consider using BGP

    D. Convert VPN to dynamic VPN

Answer: C & D

Explanation: 100 routes can be supported by a dynamic routing table. Only 50 per IPv4 and 50 per IPv6 are supported by static. So, convert VPN to dynamic VPN and consider using of BGP because BGP is the dynamic routing protocol.

324- You want to know the IP address and port of the backend instances that are serving the traffic sent from an AWS ELB. What step should you take to get this information?

    A. Enable ELB Access logs. Check the logs

    B. Check CloudWatch metrics

    C. Check the VPC Flow Logs

    D. Check the ELB Console. The data is present in the log section.

Answer: A

Explanation: Elastic Load Balancing provides access logs to collect detailed information about requests sent to your load balancer. Each log provides data such as the request received time, IP address of the client, latencies, request paths and server responses. These access logs can be used to analyze traffic patterns and to resolve problems.

325- Which of the services below can be used to mitigate DDoS attacks on your AWS application? (Choose 3)

  A. Elastic Load Balancer
  B. CloudFront
  C. Route 53
  D. SQS

Answer: **A, B, & C**

Explanation:

- Elastic Load Balancing (ELB) permits the automated distribution of application traffic across multiple Availability Zones to several Amazon Elastic Compute Cloud instances, minimizing the risk of overloading any one EC2 instance. Elastic Load Balancing supports only valid TCP requests. DDoS attacks such as UDP and SYN floods cannot reach EC2 instances

- Amazon CloudFront distributes traffic across multiple Points of Presences (PoPs) and filters applications to make sure only valid HTTP(S) requests are sent to backend hosts

- Route 53- The Domain Name System (DNS) is one of the most of frequent targets of DDoS attacks. Amazon Route 53 is a highly-available, scalable DNS service for routing end-users into AWS or outside AWS infrastructure. Route 53 enables traffic to be managed across a range of routing types globally and offers out-of-the-box shuffle sharding and Anycast routing capabilities to protect domain names from DNS-based DDoS attacks.

326- You want to change the cache behavior for objects that are stored in CloudFront. Choose 3 suitable options for this purpose.

  A. Cache TTL
  B. Default TTL
  C. Minimum TTL
  D. Maximum TTL

Answer: **B, C, & D**

Explanation: You can change the CloudFront settings of Minimum TTL, Maximum TTL and Default TTL for a cache behavior in order to change the duration of the cache for every object that matches the same path pattern.

327-   By using CloudWatch log services, which of the following tasks can be achieved? (Choose 3)

    A. Streaming of the log data to Amazon Kinesis

    B. Streaming of the log data into Amazon ElasticSearch in near real-time with CloudWatch Logs subscriptions

    C. Recording of API calls for your AWS account and delivering log files containing API calls to your Amazon S3 bucket

    D. Sending the log data to AWS Lambda for custom processing or to load into other systems

Answer: **A, B, & D**

Explanation: You can monitor, store and access your log files with Amazon CloudWatch Logs from AWS CloudTrail, EC2 instances, and other sources. The associated log data can then be retrieved from CloudWatch Logs. You can access a real-time log file from CloudWatch Logs using subscriptions, deliver it for custom processing, evaluation, or loading to other services, such as Amazon Kinesis Stream, Amazon Kinesis Data Firehose Stream, or AWS Lambda. You can setup a log group for CloudWatch Logs to transfer information received by CloudWatch Logs in almost real time into your Amazon ElasticSearch cluster.

328-   There are a number of VPCs currently hosted by a company at AWS. A VPN connection is present between your on-premises data center and your AWS. They want to restrict the number of VPN connections that would be created so that they can ensure the communication between VPC hosts and on-premises services. From the following options, select the one that meets the requirement.

    A. Create shared service VPC and route all requests to the other VPCs via this VPC

    B. There is no way to ensure that there is a VPN connection between each VPC and the on-premises infrastructure

    C. Make use of an AWS Storage Gateway to integrate AWS Cloud with existing on-premises infrastructure

    D. Peer the VPCs together and then forward the traffic through one of the VPCs

Answer: **A**

Explanation: This approach generates VPC shared services that include replicated services as well as proxies for remote resource requests that cannot be replicated as a shared service directly. This approach eliminates the need for VPN connections for additional VPCs, since all required

on-site resources are directly or indirectly accessed by the VPC shared services. This option is best for the customers who:

- Have majority of their infrastructure on AWS
- Want to limit VPN traffic
- Need on-premises resources that are easy to replicate or proxy

329-   Which of the below options represent the minimum subnet size of a VPC in AWS?

    A. /29
    B. /28
    C. /27
    D. /26

Answer: **B**

Explanation: The subnet's minimum size is /28 that gives 11 available IP addresses and 5 reserved IP addresses.

330-   How can you obtain the list of IP addresses of the Edge Server Locations for CloudFront?

    A. By contacting AWS
    B. By checking the CloudFront Console
    C. By using the CloudFront API to query the IP addresses
    D. By downloading the ip-ranges.json file available from AWS

Answer: **D**

Explanation: The current IP address ranges of Amazon Web Services (AWS) are published in JSON format. Download ip-ranges.json to view current ranges.

331-   If you want network speeds for supported instance types of up to 25 Gbps, which of the following would you be the most likely to use?

    A. Route Propagation
    B. Elastic Network Adapter
    C. VPC Peering
    D. Intel 82599 Virtual Function (VF) interface

Answer: **B**

Explanation: For some supported instance types, Elastic Network Adapter (ENA) supports network speeds of up to 25 Gbps.

332- Choose 3 options that can directly serve as authentication services for Amazon WorkSpaces.

    A. Direct Connect

    B. Simple AD

    C. Microsoft AD hosted on AWS

    D. AD Connector

Answer: **B, C, & D**

Explanation: Amazon WorkSpaces uses a directory for your work space and users to store and manage information. One of the options can be used:

- Simple AD — Create a directory that is compatible with Microsoft Active Directory, powered by Samba 4, and hosted on AWS
- Microsoft AD — Create a Microsoft Active Directory hosted on AWS
- AD Connector — Use your existing on-premises Microsoft Active Directory. Users can sign into their Work Spaces using their on-premises credentials and access on-premises resources from their Work Spaces
- Cross trust — Create a trust relationship between your Microsoft AD directory and your on-premises domain

333- Choose the option that is not available in the DHCP options' set.

    A. IP-Range

    B. domain-name-servers

    C. ntp-servers

    D. domain-name

Answer: **A**

Explanation: The DHCP supported options are domain-name-servers, domain-name, ntp-servers, netbios-name-servers, and netbios-node-type.

334- Which of the following services can protect your web applications against ordinary web exploits?

    A. AWS CloudTrail
    B. AWS SQS
    C. AWS WAF
    D. AWS Config

Answer: **C**

Explanation: AWS WAF is a firewall that protects your web applications from common web exploits, which may affect the availability of applications, compromise security or consume excessive resources. AWS WAF can be used to create custom rules that block common attack patterns, such as SQL injection or cross-site scripting, and rules that are designed for your specific application. New rules can be deployed within minutes, letting you respond quickly to changing traffic patterns. AWS WAF also includes a full - function API that can be used to automate web security rule creation, deployment, and maintenance.

335- You want to check whether the instances in private subnets are able to communicate to the internet, which of the following option would you choose? (Choose 2)

    A. AWS Direct Connect
    B. NAT Gateway
    C. Internet Gateway
    D. NAT Instances

Answer: **B & D**

Explanation: In a private subnet, customer EC2 instances sometimes have to communicate with the public internet. This connection is enabled by a NAT device, which replaces private IP addresses of internal servers with public IP addresses on the way out of the of network and translates IP addresses on the way back in. AWS offers two types of NAT options: NAT instances and NAT gateways. NAT gateways are managed by AWS while NAT instances are managed by customers. NAT gateways offer better availability and bandwidth over individual NAT instances, but customers can use multiple NAT instances to increase the availability and performance of the network.

336- Choose 2 options that are valid origins for CloudFront Web distributions.

A. An SQS Queue
B. An SNS Topic
C. An HTTP Server
D. An S3 Bucket

Answer: **C & D**
Explanation: The origin of a CloudFront distribution may be an S3 bucket or HTTP server from which CloudFront receives the files that it distributes.

337-   You have an on-premises Active Directory setup in your company. The company wants to have the ability to use their on-premises Active Directory for authentication purpose even after they have extended their footprints on AWS. You want to ensure that AWS resources can continue using the existing credentials that are stored in the on-premises Active Directory. How can this be done?

A. By using the AWS Simple AD service
B. By using the Classic Link feature on AWS
C. By using the Active Directory connector service on AWS
D. By using the Active Directory service on AWS

Answer: **C**
Explanation: AD Connector is a directory gateway that allows you to redirect requests for directories to your Microsoft Active Directory on-site without caching any Cloud data. AD Connector is available in two sizes, large and small. For smaller organizations with up to 500 users, a small AD connector is designed. A large AD Connector can support up to 5,000 users in larger organizations.

338-   A company is creating VPN connections with its on-premises data centers. Which of the given options are best steps for the company to follow? (Choose 3)

A. Ensure to implement non-overlapping network ranges for your private networks
B. Consider using static routed network connections for better performance
C. Consider using dynamic routed network connections for better performance
D. Ensure to limit the traffic that flows through the VPN

Answer: **A, C, & D**

Explanation: Some universal principles of network design must be taken into account when configuring VPN connections to any computer network. For example, limit the amount of traffic that has to go through VPN connections whenever possible. This reduces contention and latency of the VPN network, which can improve the performance of the application. In order to simplify the routing between remote networks, it is also best to implement non-overlapping network ranges for your private networks. You can use dynamically routed network connections to create highly available, resilient, scalable links to your corporate network resources.

339- When using VPC for IPv6 CIDR block, which of the following fixed allocated size would you choose?

    A. /32
    B. /40
    C. /56
    D. /64

Answer: **C**
Explanation: The VPC is a fixed size of /56 for IPv6 (in CIDR notation). A VPC can be associated with IPv4 and IPv6 CIDR blocks. While for creating subnet, /64 is the fixed size for IPv6 CIDR in VPC.

340- Which of the given statement is incorrect regarding AWS Load Balancer?

    A. The DNS name of an Internet-facing Load Balancer is publicly resolvable to the public IP addresses of the nodes
    B. The nodes of an internal Load Balancer have private IP addresses only
    C. The nodes of an Internet-facing Load Balancer have private IP addresses
    D. The nodes of an internal Load Balancer have public IP addresses only

Answer: **C**
Explanation: The nodes of a load balancer facing the internet have public IP addresses. The DNS name of a load balancer facing the internet can be publicly resolved to the nodes' public IP addresses. Internet-facing load balancers can, therefore, route customer requests over the internet.

The internal load balancer nodes only have private IP addresses. The internal load balancer's DNS name can be publicly resolved to the nodes' private IP addresses. Internal load balancers can therefore only route requests for load balancers from customers with access to the VPC.

341-   Choose the option that is the container for resource records in Route 53.

  A. Delegation Set
  B. Hosted Zone
  C. Name Server
  D. Domain Name

Answer: **B**

Explanation: It is a container for sets of resource records, which contain information on how to route traffic to a domain (such as example.com) and all its subdomains (such as www.example.com, retail.example.com, and seattle.accounting.example.com). A hosted zone has the same name as the corresponding domain.

342-   Indicate the port number that is used by HTTPS protocol.

  A. 443
  B. 80
  C. 23
  D. 22

Answer: **A**

Explanation: HTTPS URLs begin with "https://" and by default use port 443, whereas HTTP URLs begin with "http://" and by default use port 80.

343-   Choose 2 options that are valid VPC CIDRs.

  A. 10.0.0.0/29
  B. 10.0.0.0/24
  C. 20.0.0.0/27
  D. 20.0.0.0/10

Answer: **B & C**

Explanation: You must specify an IPv4 CIDR block for the VPC when creating a VPC. The block size allowed is between a netmask / 16 (65,536 IP addresses) and a netmask / 28 (16 IP addresses).

344- Which of the given statement is false about VPC and IP addressing?

    A. You cannot disable IPv4 support for your VPC
    B. The default IP addressing for Amazon VPC and Amazon EC2 is IPv4
    C. You can enable IPv6 support for your VPC and resources
    D. You can only operate VPCs in one mode at a time, either IPv4 or IPv6

Answer: **D**

Explanation: You can enable IPv6 support for your VPC and resources if you have an existing VPC that only supports IPv4, and resources in your subnet that is configured to use IPv4 only. Your VPC can work in dual-stack mode - your resources can communicate via IPv4, IPv6 or both. Communication between IPv4 and IPv6 is independent. You cannot deactivate IPv4 support for your VPC and subnets; this is the Amazon VPC and Amazon EC2 IP addressing system.

345- Choose the false statement about DHCP options sets.

    A. If you delete a VPC, the DHCP options sets associated with the VPC are also deleted
    B. You can have multiple sets of DHCP options
    C. You can modify the DHCP options sets after they have been created
    D. One DHCP options set can be associated with one VPC at a time

Answer: **C**

Explanation: You cannot modify DHCP options after creating a set of DHCP options. You have to create a new set and associate it with your VPC if you want that your VPC uses a different set of DHCP options. You have to set up your VPC to use no DHCP options at all.

346- Select two types of endpoints that are available in a VPC in order to access Public AWS resources.

    A. Internal
    B. Gateway
    C. Primary
    D. Interface

Answer: **B & D**

Explanation: Gateway Endpoint - A gateway that is a target for a specified route in your route table, used for traffic destined to a supported AWS service.

Interface Endpoint - An elastic network interface with a private IP address that serves as an entry point for traffic destined to a supported AWS service.

347-   An audit will be performed for the AWS account of your company. What steps given below will ensure that the auditor has the correct access to your AWS account logs?

   A. Ensure that CloudTrail is enabled. Create a user for the IT Auditor and ensure that full control is given to the user for CloudTrail

   B. Ensure that CloudTrail is enabled. Create a role for read-only access to CloudTrail. Create a user for the IT Auditor and attach the role to the user

   C. Enable CloudWatch Logs. Create a user for the IT Auditor and ensure that full control is given to the user for the CloudWatch Logs

   D. Enable S3 and ELB logs. Send the logs as a zip file to the IT Auditor

Answer: **B**

Explanation: AWS CloudTrail is an AWS service that enables your AWS accounts to be governed, complied with, operated, and risk audited. User, role or AWS service actions are recorded in CloudTrail as events. Events include AWS Management Console, AWS Command Line Interface, AWS SDK and API actions. The best option to provide right access to AWS account logs is by using roles with appropriate permission and then attaching them to the specific user who wants that permission.

348-   To ensure that the instances in your private subnet can download updates from the internet, you have set up a NAT gateway. However, even after the gateway has been established, instances still cannot access the internet. From the given options, which is the wrong procedure to diagnose the problem?

   A. Verify that the NAT gateway has been created in the public subnet

   B. Verify that the NAT gateway is in the Available state

   C. Make sure that the private subnet's route table has a default route pointing to the NAT gateway

   D. Verify that the destination is reachable by pinging the destination from another source using a public IP address

Answer: **A**

Explanation: In the public subnet, the NAT gateway must be created not in the private subnet. Below mentioned points can be used to troubleshoot internet connectivity issues for EC2 instance:

- Make sure that the destination is reached using a public IP address by pinging the destination from another source
- Check that the NAT gateway is in the state of availability. Note: After about an hour, a NAT gateway in the Failed State is automatically removed
- Make sure your NAT gateway has been created in a public subnet and that the public route table has a default route pointing to an internet gateway
- Make sure the route table of the private subnet has a default route pointing to the NAT gateway

349- For default VPC's setup in AWS, default CIDR range is _____.

    A. 192.168.0.0/16
    B. 20.0.0.0/16
    C. 10.0.0.0/16
    D. 172.31.0.0/16

Answer: **D**

Explanation: A CIDR range of 172.31.0.0/16 is assigned to default VPCs. Default VPC subnets have /20 netblocks assigned for the VPC CIDR range.

350- Which of the AWS services are used to monitor any changes to the network configuration of the VPCs and subnets in AWS?

    A. AWS CloudWatch Logs
    B. AWS Config
    C. AWS CloudTrail
    D. AWS Direct Connect

Answer: **A, B, & C**

Explanation: AWS CloudTrail provides an account history of AWS API calls, including API calls via the AWS Management Console, AWS SDKs, command line tools and AWS services of higher

level (such as AWS CloudFormation). This call history of the AWS API allows security analysis, resource change tracking, and compliance auditing. Customers can also provide CloudTrail data to CloudWatch Logs for storing, monitoring and processing API calls for network - specific changes and sending appropriate notifications. AWS Config generates an inventory of AWS network resource, including the configuration history and notification for configuration changes.

351-   Among the given options, select two types of MTU supported by instance types in AWS.

   A. 9001
   B. 5001
   C. 1500
   D. 2001

Answer: **A & C**

Explanation: All Amazon EC2 instance types support 1500 MTU, and many current instance sizes support 9001 MTU or jumbo frames.

352-   You want to check that your subnet is able to receive requests from all destinations. Which of the given options will you use in your route table?

   A. 0.0.0.0/32
   B. 255.255.255.255/0
   C. 0.0.0.0/0
   D. 255.255.255.255/32

Answer: **C**

Explanation: It is the default route that allows our subnet to receive traffic from anywhere.

353-   You need a cost-effective solution in the cloud to host your AD data. You want to use it by using Work Space, rather than having all the features of AD. What is the best solution from the following options?

   A. Use the Hosted Microsoft AD solution
   B. Consider using the AD Connector
   C. Use the Simple AD solution

D. Deploy an AD server on an M3.large instance

Answer: **C**

Explanation: Amazon WorkSpaces uses directories to store and manage WorkSpaces and user's information. You can choose from the Simple AD, AD Connector or AWS Directory Service for Microsoft Active Directory (Enterprise Edition), also known as Microsoft AD, for your directory. You can also establish a relationship of trust between your Microsoft AD directory and your on-premises domain.

354-   Which of the following items are you unable to capture via VPC Flow Logs?

A. Frames
B. Destination Port
C. Source Address
D. Packets

Answer: **A**

Explanation: You can capture version, account-id, interface-id, source address, destination address, source port, destination port, protocols, and packets via VPC Flow Logs.

355-   You want to monitor the traffic for your EC2 instance. Which of the given options would provide you with this feature?

A. NACLs
B. VPC Flow Logs
C. Subnet Flow Logs
D. Security Groups

Answer: **B**

Explanation: Flow Logs help you with a number of tasks, such as troubleshooting the reason for why specific traffic does not reach an instance, which can help you to diagnose excessively restrictive security group rules. Flow Logs can also be used to monitor traffic in your instance as a security tool.

356- If you want to ensure that the instances of VPC subnets can access the internet, what are the requirements other than the mentioned two aspects?

- Ensure that your subnet's route table points to the internet gateway
- Ensure that your network access control and security group rules allow the relevant traffic to flow to and from your instance

Choose 2 answers.

    A. Ensure that the instance in the subnet has a public IP

    B. Attach an internet gateway to your subnet

    C. Attach an internet gateway to your VPC

    D. Ensure that the instance in the subnet has a private IP

Answer: **A & C**

Explanation: You must do the following in order to enable access to or from the internet, for instances in a VPC subnet:

- Attach an Internet gateway to your VPC
- Make sure the route table of your subnet points to the internet gateway
- Make sure that your subnet instances have a unique IP address that is global (public IPv4 address, Elastic IP address or IPv6 address)
- Make sure your Network Access Control List and security group rules allow the relevant traffic to flow to your instance and from your instance

357- Which of the following services can be used for a snapshot of the current configuration of the resources in an AWS account?

    A. AWS Trusted Advisor

    B. AWS IAM

    C. AWS Code Deploy

    D. AWS Config

Answer: **D**

Explanation: You can do this with AWS Config:

- Get a snapshot of the current support resources configurations associated with your AWS account
- Recover settings of one or more resources in your account
- Retrieve one or more historical resource configurations
- When a resource is created, modified or deleted, receive a notification

- View resource relationships. For example, you may want to find all resources that use a specific security group

358- You are working in a company that has a Direct Connect solution with high availability that utilizes two data centers. Each of them contains one two-connection LAG and one standard DX connection. If your company completes an order to add a new connection to each LAG, how many LOAs will be filled out in total?

    A. 1
    B. 2
    C. 4
    D. 6

Answer: **C**

Explanation: LOA is used for DX and Link, Aggregation. In this example, every data center would have 2 LOAs (1 DX and 1 LAG) = 4 for 2 data centers and the addition of a connection to the LAGs added will not increase the LOAs number.

When creating a LAG, the Letter of Authorization and Connecting Facility Assignment (LOA - CFA) can be downloaded from the AWS Direct Connect console for each new physical connection.

359- Which of the following has the Elastic IP property?

    A. MAC Address
    B. CloudTrail
    C. Subnet
    D. Elastic Network Interface

Answer: **D**

Explanation: An Elastic IP address is a network interface property. By updating the network interface attached to the instance, you can associate an Elastic IP address with an instance. Given below is the list of network interface attributes:

- A MAC addresses
- One public IPv4 address
- One Elastic IP address (IPv4) per private IPv4 address
- One or more secondary private IPv4 addresses

- A description
- One or more IPv6 addresses
- A source/destination check flag
- One or more security groups
- A primary private IPv4 address

360- Choose 3 options that are pre-requisites for using the AD connector available in AWS.

    A. The VPC must have default hardware tenancy

    B. The VPC must have shared tenancy

    C. The VPC must be connected to your on-premises network

    D. There should be at least 2 subnets in the VPC with each in a different availability zone

Answer: **A, C, & D**

Explanation: VPC should be set up with following pre-requisites as mentioned below:

- The VPC must have default hardware tenancy
- The VPC must be connected to your on-premises network through a Virtual Private Network (VPN) connection or AWS Direct Connect
- At least two subnets. Each of the subnets must be in a different Availability Zone

361- Choose the option that represents the number of DHCP options set that can be assigned to a VPC at a time.

    A. 8

    B. 4

    C. 2

    D. 1

Answer: **D**

Explanation: You can have several sets of DHCP options, but only one DHCP option set can be associated with a VPC at the same time.

362- A company has three VPCs:

- VPC-A (10.0.0.0/16)

- VPC-B (10.1.0.0/16)
- VPC-C (10.1.0.0/16)

To ensure the communication between VPC-A and other VPCs, choose two options that would provide the solution for the mentioned task.

    A. This cannot be done because of the overlapping CIDR blocks

    B. Ensure the route tables are modified with the new peering connections

    C. Create a VPC peering relationship between VPC-A and VPC-B and between VPC-B and VPC-C

    D. Create a VPC peering relationship between VPC-A and VPC-B and between VPC-A and VPC-C

Answer: **B & D**

Explanation: It is necessary to update the route tables of all the peered VPCs. VPCs do not support transitive routing, therefore, VPC A should be peered separately with VPC A and VPC B.

363- Choose 3 traffic types that are not captured by the VPC flow logs.

    A. IP traffic going to and from network interfaces

    B. Traffic generated by instances when they contact the Amazon DNS server

    C. DHCP traffic

    D. Traffic to and from 169.254.169.254

Answer: **B, C, & D**

Explanation: Some points on the types of traffic not captured by VPC Flow Logs are:

- Instances generated traffic when contacting the Amazon DNS server. If you use your own DNS server, all DNS server traffic is logged
- A Windows instance generated traffic to activate the Amazon Windows license
- For instance, metadata traffic to and from 169.254.169.254
- DHCP traffic
- Traffic to the default VPC router's reserved IP address

364- What is the equivalent Network mask for a CIDR block (10.0.0.0/24)?

    A. 255.255.255.0

    B. 255.255.252.0

    C. 255.255.250.0

D. 255.255.254.0

Answer: **A**

Explanation: Since the CIDR block belongs to Class C, for network mask, put all network bits to 1's and host bits to 0's so its 255.255.255.0.

365- You have to upload information to an S3 bucket for multiple EC2 instances deployed from Amazon AMIs. The public internet should not pass through this information. The instances must be updated as well. What is the best option for this?

A. Use an S3 endpoint along with a NAT gateway
B. Consider using a VPN with an IP address specified in the AWS official S3 prefix list
C. Use an S3 endpoint associated with the VPC
D. Use an S3 endpoint along with a NAT Instance

Answer: **C**

Explanation: Options A and D are wrong because both the NAT gateway and NAT instance are used for private instances to communicate with the internet.

Option B is wrong as VPN is not a solution for this case hence, option C is right. The main requirement of the question is that information must be uploaded to S3 using the internet. S3 is a service outside the VPC. The server must also be updated with the latest patches.

NAT Gateway is not required because AWS hosts the YUM repository on S3 can be accessed using the S3 VPC gateway endpoint and does not need to go over the internet to update the server.

We have to create a VPC S3 endpoint and select the route table.

This endpoint can be accessed by subnets associated with selected route tables. When we connect to an S3 endpoint, we use the internal network of Amazon to communicate with the S3 instead of the internet.

366- Identify the false statement about the NAT gateway.

A. A NAT gateway supports bursts of up to 10 Gbps of bandwidth
B. You can associate a security group with the NAT gateway
C. A NAT gateway supports the following protocols: TCP, UDP, and ICMP
D. You can associate exactly one Elastic IP address with a NAT gateway

Answer: **B**

Explanation: Characteristics of NAT gateway:

- A NAT gateway supports bandwidth bursts up to 10 Gbps. If you need more than 10 Gbps bursts, you can divide the workload into multiple subnets and create a NAT gateway in each subnet
- Exactly one Elastic IP address can be associated with a NAT gateway. After it is created, you cannot separate an Elastic IP address from a NAT gateway. You must create a new NAT gateway with the required address to use a different Elastic IP address for your NAT gateway, update your route tables and delete the existing NAT gateway if it is no longer required
- The following protocols are supported by a NAT Gateway: TCP, UDP and ICMP
- You cannot connect a NAT gateway to a security group. To control the traffic to and from such instances, use security groups for your instances in private subnet

367-   What does it mean when one wants to configure white-label servers in AWS?

   A. This is when you want to configure placement groups for the first time
   B. This is when you want to configure AMI's for EC2 Instances
   C. This is when you want to have nameservers in Route 53 to be the same as the domain name of your hosted zone
   D. This is when you want to configure EC2 Instances for the first time

Answer: **C**

Explanation: Each zone hosted by Amazon Route 53 is associated with four nameservers, collectively known as a delegation set. The nameservers have names such as ns-2048.awsdns-64.com by default. If you want your nameserver's domain name to be the same as your host zone's domain name, such as ns1.example.com, you can set up white label nameservers, also known as vanity nameservers or private nameservers.

368-   Choose the maximum bandwidth that is supported for the Link Aggregation Group when it comes to Direct Connect. (Choose 2)

   A. 20 Gbps
   B. 10 Gbps
   C. 1 Gbps
   D. 500 Mbps

Answer: **B**

Explanation: For Link Aggregation Group, the same bandwidth must be used for all LAG connections. Support for the following bandwidths: 1 Gbps and 10 Gbps. In a LAG, you can have up to 4 connections. Each LAG connection counts towards the overall limit of the region's connection. All LAG connections must terminate at the same endpoint of AWS Direct Connect.

369-   A company has two VPCs that need to be connected via VPC peering. Which routes should be added in the table so that both VPCs can communicate with each other. The target of VPC peering is pcx-4321. (Choose 2)

    A. In the Route table for VPCB add a route of VPCB and Target as pcx-4321
    B. In the Route table for VPCB add a route of VPCA and Target as pcx-4321
    C. In the Route table for VPCA add a route of VPCA and Target as pcx-4321
    D. In the Route table for VPCA add a route of VPCB and Target as pcx-4321

Answer: **B & D**

Explanation: If two VPCs have VPC peering between them, then in both the VPC's route table, you need to add VPC CIDR value as a destination and VPC peer ID as a target.

370-   An organization has a VPC in which application is hosted on instances but some errors occur again and again, so the organization needs to trace packets sent from the application to identify the issue. How can this be done?

    A. By using CloudWatch Logs
    B. By using VPC Flow logs
    C. By using CloudTrail
    D. By using an IDS

Answer: **D**

Explanation: In order to do packet-level analyzation, use IDS to detect the error.

371-   John has VPC in his AWS in which instances are configured for querying the on-premises data center DNS server. However, he is unable to communicate with the on-premises server. What might be the issue? (Choose 2)

    A. The NACLs are blocking incoming on port 53 for UDP

B. The NACLs are blocking incoming on port 53 for TCP

C. The Security Groups for the EC2 Instances are blocking incoming on port 53

D. The NACLs are blocking outgoing on port 53 for UDP

E. The NACLs are blocking outgoing on port 53 for TCP

Answer: **D & E**

Explanation: For communication with DNS server, instances need to reach DNS server via port 53 for both TCP and UDP. We may conclude that in NACL, these two are blocked and this is why John is unable to communicate with DNS.

372- A company has a VPC with the private and public subnet. Instances in private subnet require software updates from the internet, so NAT gateway is placed in VPC but still private subnet instances are unable to communicate with the internet. What might be the reason behind this?

A. The NAT gateway has been created in the private subnet

B. The NAT gateway has been created with the wrong Instance type

C. The NAT gateway has been created in the public subnet

D. The NAT gateway has not been created with the right AMI

Answer: **A**

Explanation: If private subnet instances are unable to connect to the internet via NAT gateway, then verify the following:

• The destination is pingable using Public IP

• NAT gateway is in available state

• NAT gateway is in public subnet

• Private subnet has a route that points to NAT gateway

373- An organization has a VPC in which subnets along with instances are created. Now, the organization wants the resources to be capable of resolving on-premises DNS resources. How can this be done?

A. By creating an EC2 Instance in VPC, which will act as the DNS server

B. By creating a private hosted zone in Route 53

C. By configuring DHCP Options for the Subnet to point to the EC2 Instance

D. By configuring DHCP Options for VPC to point to the EC2 Instance

Answer: **A & D**

Explanation: For DNS resolving, you need to create an instance that acts as DNS server then on that instance, configure DHCP option so that it acts as DNS resolver and resolve the on-premises DNS resources.

374- An organization has an on-premises network and AWS VPC, and send traffic among them via VPN configuration. The VPC CIDR is 10.0.0.0/16 and subnet 10.0.1.0/20, while on-premises network CIDR is 10.0.37.0/20. Now, the organization observes that when traffic is sent from subnet to on-premises, some data is lost. What could be the reason behind this?

    A. The MTU is not set to 9001

    B. The "Do not fragment" is set in the IP header

    C. There is an overlap in prefixes

    D. You have not set Enhanced Networking on the Instances

Answer: **C**

Explanation: As per the given question, there is an instance in the subnet with IP of 10.0.1.4 and 10.0.1.5 and an instance in the subnet with IP of 10.0.1.0/20. Now, the instances in VPC are trying to communicate with the host in an on-premises network; the IP of the on-premises network is 10.0.37.0/20, which is part of the larger prefix assigned to VPC, so traffic is dropped. But if host address is 10.1.38.0/20, then it is able to communicate because this block is not part of the VPC address.

375- A company has NGINX web server running on port 80 on each EC2 instance but users are still unable to access the server running on port 80. What could be the issue?

    A. The Security Group does not allow inbound traffic on ephemeral ports

    B. The NACL does not allow inbound traffic on ephemeral ports

    C. The NACL does not allow outbound traffic on ephemeral ports

    D. The Security Group does not allow outbound traffic on port 80

Answer: **C**

Explanation: As we know that when a connection is established on a client, you need to ensure that outbound traffic is enabled for any ephemeral port for the client. The ephemeral concept is a concept on NACL. The ephemeral port is the port that is chosen by the client when it wants to initiate a request to the instance in VPC. The range of these port depends on Client OS. By using

this port, the request generated to the destination address or in response to this request is sent outside the VPC to the client address on an ephemeral port.

376-   A company uses Route 53 and for that, they configured routing policies to create a record set for a group of web servers in VPC. When any user tries to access resource record, they are able to access any web server's record in VPC. Which routing policy should be configured so that they will get a value addition in the network?

    A. Failover
    B. Simple
    C. Multi Value
    D. Weighted

Answer: **C**

Explanation: As users can get any of the resource records of any web server, then multi-value routing policy is configured that returns multiple values in response to DNS queries.

377-   An organization has an on-premises network and a VPC. It uses AWS Direct Connect connection to connect VPC and on-premises network. Which of the given sets of resources would help the company to achieve maximum fault tolerance and maximum bandwidth all time?

    A. One Virtual Private Gateway, one AWS Direct Connect Location, one VPN connection, and two Customer gateways
    B. Two Virtual Private Gateway, one AWS Direct Connect Location, and one Customer gateway
    C. Two Virtual Private Gateway, two AWS Direct Connect Locations, and one Customer gateway
    D. One Virtual Private Gateway, two AWS Direct Connect Locations, and two Customer gateways

Answer: **D**

Explanation: For high availability and fault tolerance, you can use one VGW because there is only one IGW per VPC, two AWS Direct Connect locations, and two Customer Gateways. Through this architecture, you will get high bandwidth all time and HA as well.

378- You have a multicast-based application that needs to be moved to AWS VPC network with minimal effort. How would you do this?

    A. By enabling encryption on the underlying EBS volumes that will be used to support the EC2 Instance

    B. By creating an overlay network between EC2 Instances and then exporting the application

    C. The application needs to be changed to support unicast before moving it to AWS

    D. By creating EC2 Instances in the subnet and then migrating the application on to the EC2 Instance

Answer: **B**

Explanation: In VPC currently, multicast or broadcast traffic is not allowed. So, you can use GRE tunnel to create mesh VPN overlay network for the application moving to other EC2 instances.

379- An organization has its AWS account on which AWS Direct Connect connection is used. One of its employee's account is under parent organization account, and he wants to use AWS Direct Connect connection as hosted VIF. Then what charges does the company have to pay in this case?

    A. Port hours

    B. All data transfer in

    C. Initial connection charges

    D. All data transfer out

Answer: **D**

Explanation: In AWS Direct Connect, you only need to pay for the data that are transferred out; you do not need to pay for data transfer in nor any connection charges. While port charges are carried by the parent account.

380- A government firm uses AWS S3 to save its private file and uses AWS CloudFront for serving private content from S3 by putting S3 as the origin. Now, the firm wants these contents to be restricted for individuals. What can be used to achieve this?

    A. Security Group

    B. Private Keys

C. Signed URLs

D. Signed Cookies

Answer: C

Explanation: For restricted access to the individual files, signed URLs are the best option to choose. In case of RTMP distribution, signed cookies are not supported hence signed URLs are used.

381- An organization wants to host its applications in AWS with their respective Domain name, and both applications has web server instances. Now, the organization needs HA of web servers and Route 53 configurations. How would this be done?

A. By creating a private Elastic Load Balancer

B. By creating a public Elastic Load Balancer

C. By configuring 2 private hosted zones in Route 53

D. By configuring 2 public hosted zones in Route 53

Answer: B & D

Explanation: As per requirement, there are two applications that have separate domains, so there is need to host two public zones in Route 53. A Web server instances are internet facing so, there is need of public subnet on which ELB needs to be created. Traffic is routed from the public to the webservers.

382- There is a VPN connection to 2 VPCs with same CGW for both. The CIDR of these VPCs are overlapping. How can the right routing be done to ensure that data is routed in the right path to the customer side?

A. By using BFD technology for routing

B. By using VRF technology for routing

C. By configuring AS_PATH for each of the routes

D. By using static routes on the customer side

Answer: B

Explanation: By using VRF, you can allow multiple instances to co-exist within the same router at the same time. Because instances are independent in this routing, you can connect one CGW to multiple VPCs by using VRFs.

383- An organization has 100 users and uses AWS Workspaces, but now it wants to use directory service with AWS Workspaces. How can this be done in a cost effective way with minimum administrative overhead?

A. By choosing AWS Directory Service to use along with AWS Workspaces
B. By choosing Simple AD to use along with AWS Workspaces
C. By choosing an AD connector to use along with AWS Workspaces
D. By deploying an AD domain server in a VPC and configuring AWS Workspace to use the newly created AD domain server

Answer: **B**

Explanation: To manage the information and storing of the information of workspaces and users, AWS WorkSpaces uses directories. So, you can use Simple AD, AD Connector or AWS Directory service. Using Simple AD is an ideal and less administrative overhead.

384- A company has a VPC in which EC2 instances are hosted over IPv6 protocol, and now it wants that only traffic from instance should flow to the internet but instance should not get the traffic from the internet. How can this requirement be achieved?

A. By using an Egress only Internet gateway
B. By changing the NACLs to not allow Inbound Traffic on the Instances
C. By changing the Security Groups to not allow inbound traffic on the instances
D. By changing the Internet gateway to only allow outbound traffic for IPv6

Answer: **A**

Explanation: IPv6 is globally unique and is a public resource. If there is a requirement to restrict the public resources not to access the instances, then use Egress only internet gateway that only allows instances to communicate to the internet but not allow the internet to communicate to that instance.

385- An organization has EC2 instances and an on-premises server. It wants to send packets from instance to server over the internet. Although jumbo frames set is used, the drops in packets occur because of their size. How can you, as a network specialist, overcome this?

A. By enabling Enhanced Networking on the Instance
B. By ensuring that the "Do Not Fragment" flag is not set in the IP header

C. By ensuring that the "Do Not Fragment" flag is set in the IP header

D. By ensuring that the MTU is set to 9001

Answer: **B**

Explanation: In jumbo frames, more than 1500 bytes of data is allowed as per packet size is increasing. But outside the AWS region, VPC peering allows maximum 1500 MTU. VPN supports a limit of 1500 MTU over the internet so if the packet size is more than 1500, then they are fragmented and dropped because "Do Not Fragment" flag is not set in IP header.

386- A company uses Route 53 health checks for its 2 on-premises web servers but health checks are failed again and again. How can this issue be solved?

A. This is not possible. You cannot enable health checks for non-AWS resources

B. By ensuring that the Firewall on your on-premises environment is allowing inbound traffic

C. By ensuring that the NACLs on the Subnets are allowing inbound traffic

D. By ensuring that the Security Groups on the instances are allowing inbound traffic

Answer: **B**

Explanation: In Route 53, when you check the health of endpoint, it sends HTTP, HTTPS or TCP request to IP address or port that is defined at configuring health. So, there is a need that your router and firewall must allow inbound traffic from IP address that the health checker uses.

387- An organization needs to use VPN connection for which it sets up a VPN software on the instance. What is the other thing that needs to be done?

A. Enable enhanced networking mode on the Amazon EC2 instance

B. Enable route propagation in a Virtual Private Cloud (VPC) subnet route table

C. Enable source destination check on the Amazon EC2 instance

D. Disable source destination check on the Amazon EC2 instance

Answer: **D**

Explanation: To launch VPN instance, you need to ensure that the following things are set:

- Instance must be launched in public subnet
- Source destination checks on the instance must be disabled

388-   An organization uses software to track the IP traffic flow in its on-premises systems, and now it wants to do the same in AWS. Which service can be used for this purpose?

   A. AWS Config
   B. AWS CloudWatch logs
   C. AWS VPC Flow Logs
   D. AWS CloudWatch metrics

Answer: **C**

Explanation: In AWS, they can use VPC Flow Logs to track IP traffic. Logs include source IP, Destination IP, ports, protocol, packets, Allow/Deny actions for ENI, VPC, and subnet.

389-   An organization is using Route 53 for hosted zones but it wants the hosted zone nameserver to resemble its domain name. How can this requirement be achieved?

   A. By creating a Reusable delegation set using the AWS CLI
   B. By creating a Reusable delegation set using Route 53 API's
   C. By creating a Reusable deletion set using the AWS Console
   D. By specifying the domain name when creating the record set for the nameservers

Answer: **A & B**

Explanation: In Amazon Route 53, each hosted zone is associated with four nameservers, known collectively as a delegation set. By default, the nameservers have names, but if you want the domain name of your nameservers to be the same as the domain name of your hosted zone, then you can configure white label nameservers, also known as vanity nameservers or private nameservers. To create reusable delegation set, use APIs or AWS CLIs or SDKs.

390-   An organization has an application running on EC2 instances, Application Load Balancer and CloudFront. If a DDoS attack occurs, then how would the organization prevent itself from this network attack? (Choose 3)

   A. By using AWS Shield Advanced
   B. By placing the AWS WAF in front of the CloudFront Distribution
   C. By placing the AWS WAF in front of the Application Load Balancer
   D. By placing the AWS WAF in front of the EC2 Instances

Answer: **A, B, & C**

Explanation: WAF is used for monitoring HTTP, or HTTPs requests sent to CloudFront and Application Load Balancer while AWS Shield Advanced provides DDoS protection to instances, ELB, Route 53, and ELB, but it has some additional charges.

391- A company has an application that uses EC2 instance for frontend part and for processing of images. Now, the company want to use ELB to forward the request based on the type and then route it to its respective servers. How can they this requirement be achieved? (Choose 2)

A. By creating a TCP Listener
B. By creating an Application Load Balancer
C. By creating different target groups
D. By creating Classic Load Balancer

Answer: **B & C**

Explanation: To route traffic on the basis of request type, you can use Application Load Balancer and the target group of each instance.

392- An organization has network design in which it uses EC2 instance within a VPC that needs to communicate to both public and private subnet and also wants that traffic from private subnet to be sent only to the Central EC2 instance. How do you, as a network design engineer, fulfill this requirement?

A. By attaching a secondary ENI to the Instance
B. By attaching an elastic IP to the Instance
C. By attaching a public and private IP to the instance
D. By assigning a secondary IP to the ENI attached to the EC2 Instance

Answer: **A**

Explanation: According to the scenario described in the question, the instance is acting as management instance so for that, you need to create a separate Elastic Network Interface (ENI). This ENI is associated with a separate subnet inside VPC that has more restrictions. So, you need to create a secondary ENI as one ENI is already attached to an instance in public subnet. Attach this secondary ENI to another subnet that contains the management instance.

393- Your company has a VPN connection as backup, and AWS Direct Connect connection as a first priority. As a network design engineer how would you know that AWS Direct Connect is the preferred path?

    A. By ensuring that the shortest prefix is advertised on AWS Direct Connect
    B. By ensuring that AS_PATH prepending is configured on AWS Direct Connect
    C. By ensuring that the longest prefix is advertised on AWS Direct Connect
    D. By ensuring that prefixes are advertised the same way on both connections

Answer: **D**

Explanation: When you want to configure VPN as a backup path for AWS Direct Connect using VPN and AWS Direct Connect connection, then:

- Be sure that you use the same virtual private gateway for both Direct Connect and the VPN connection to the VPC
- If you are advertising the same routes toward the AWS VPC, the Direct Connect path is always preferred, regardless of AS path prepending
- If you are configuring a Border Gateway Protocol (BGP) VPN, advertise the same prefix for Direct Connect and the VPN
- If you are configuring a static VPN, add the same static prefixes to the VPN connection that you are announcing with the Direct Connect Virtual Interface

394- An organization has its on-premises environment and wants to move files from there to S3. It also wants the on-premises environment to access files with low latency. How would this be done?

    A. By creating a VPN connection along with a VPC endpoint
    B. By creating a Direct Connect connection along with a Private VIF
    C. By creating a Direct Connect connection along with a Public VIF
    D. By creating a VPN connection that would allow the services on premise to access S3

Answer: **C**

Explanation: For connecting to AWS public services like S3 or EC2, then use public VIF (Virtual Interface) with AWS Direct Connect.

395- How do you, as network design engineer, make underlying instances' performance high and communication among them enhanced within a VPC?

    A. By creating the instances in the same Availability Zone and putting them in a cluster placement Group

    B. By creating the instances in separate Availability Zones and putting them in a cluster placement Group

    C. By setting the MTU for the instances to 1500

    D. By enabling Enhanced Networking for the underlying instances

Answer: **A & D**

Explanation: Cluster placement groups use a grouping of instances within single AZ. It provides low latency and high network performance. If you need the lowest latency and the highest number of the packet within a placement group, then use enhanced networking for underlying instances.

396- A company has VPC hosted in AWS. There is a private zone hosted inside VPC for instances. Now on-premises server needs to resolve the DNS request for instances in VPC with minimal efforts. How would this be done? (Choose 2)

    A. By making your on-premises servers point to the new Domain Controller

    B. By making your on-premises servers point to the Simple AD Instance

    C. By setting up an Active Directory Domain Controller in the AWS VPC

    D. By setting up a Simple AD Instance in AWS

Answer: **B & D**

Explanation: By using Simple AD, you allowed the DNS request to be forwarded to the IP address of Amazon-provided DNS servers in VPC. Now, DNS servers will resolve names configured in your Route 53 private hosted zones. By pointing your on-premises computers to your Simple AD, you can now resolve DNS requests to the private hosted zone.

397- An organization has three VPCs; two VPCs in the same account and one VPC in another account. The organization wants the traffic from VPC A flow to VPC B, then from VPC B to VPC. As a network design engineer, what will you do to fulfill this requirement?

    A. Create a VPC Peering connection between VPC A and VPC B. Create a VPN connection between VPC B and VPC C

B. Create a VPC Peering connection between VPC A and VPC C. Create a VPN connection between VPC A and VPC B

C. Create a VPC Peering connection between VPC A and VPC B. Create another VPC peering connection between VPC B and VPC C

D. Create a VPC Peering connection between VPC A and VPC C. Create another VPC peering connection between VPC B and VPC C

Answer: **A**

Explanation: VPC peering does not follow transitive property, so by creating the VPC peering connection between VPCs that are in the same account and a VPN between VPC B and VPC C that are in the different account.

398- An organization needs to use AWS Direct Connect connection in AWS but is not capable of facilitating 1Gbps connection. How can the company achieve sub-1G connection? (Choose 2)

A. By contacting an AWS Partner for a Hosted Connection

B. By contacting an AWS Partner for a Hosted Virtual Interface

C. By having a Hosted Virtual Interface if the company has a parent AWS Account that can accommodate a 1G connection

D. By having a Hosted Connection if the company has a parent AWS Account that can accommodate a 1G connection

Answer: **A & C**

Explanation: Hosted VIF works same as standard VIFS to connect to public resource except if hosted VIF account is different from connection owner. Hosted connections allow an APN partner to create a Direct Connect sub-1G connection for you, allocating dedicated bandwidth for that connection rather than having multiple VIFs on the same parent connection competing for bandwidth.

399- An educational institute has an application hosted on a set of EC2 instances placed behind an ELB that communicates with the legacy protocol. Now, the institute wants that traffic between its users and EC2 instances to be secure. How can these requirements be fulfilled?

A. By using a Classic Load Balancer and terminating the SSL connection at the EC2 instances

B. By using an Application Load Balancer and terminating the SSL connection at the EC2 instances

C. By using a Classic Load Balancer and terminating the SSL connection at the ELB

D. By using an Application Load Balancer and terminating the SSL connection at the ELB

Answer: **A**

Explanation: As the question said that application using legacy protocol then ELB is used at network layer, so Classic Load Balancer is appropriate to choose and for secure traffic to the EC2 instances, SSL termination is needed on instances.

400-   An organization has two VPCs with AD domains. VPC peering is established between them but the joining of AD domain is not established. How can the organization make sure that AD domain joins work as planned?

A. By ensuring that the AD is placed in a public subnet

B. By ensuring the security groups for AD hosted instance has the right rules for relevant instances

C. By changing the VPC peering connection to a Direct Connect connection

D. By changing the VPC peering connection to a VPN connection

Answer: **B**

Explanation: For AD joining, security groups for AD instances have right rules to allow incoming traffic in it. AD is always in private subnet.

401-   A company has some interfaces from which it wants to delete unwanted interface manually, but is unable to delete it. What could be the reason?

"Status": "in-use",

    ...

    "Description": "VPC Endpoint Interface vpce-089f2123488812123",

    "NetworkInterfaceId": "eni-c8fbc27e",

    "VpcId": "vpc-1a2b3c4d",

    "PrivateIpAddresses": [

        {

            "PrivateDnsName": "ip-10-0-2-227.ec2.internal",

```
        "Primary": true,
        "PrivateIpAddress": "10.0.2.227"
      }
    ],
    "RequesterManaged": true,
    ...
  }
```

A. Its attached to a VPC
B. It has a private IP address attached
C. It has a private DNS name attached
D. It is a requester managed interface

Answer: **D**

Explanation: If the interface is requester managed interface, then it cannot detach or modify. This interface is created by AWS service in VPC for representing the instance for another service like RDS etc. If you delete that resource for which network interface is created, then AWS service detaches and deletes that interface.

402- You have a set of instances inside a VPC, and you want to monitor all API calls and traffic flows on instances. How would you perform the monitoring?

A. AWS CloudTrail and AWS Config
B. AWS CloudTrail and CloudWatch Logs
C. AWS CloudTrail and VPC Flow Logs
D. Amazon CloudWatch Logs and VPC Flow Logs

Answer: **C**

Explanation: For the monitoring of API calls, you can use AWS CloudTrail service while for the monitoring of IP traffic flow in VPC, you can use VPC Flow Logs.

403- For AWS Direct Connect connection, which option is not needed in the setup?

A. VLAN Encapsulation
B. Single Mode Fiber

C. Support for the router for BGP

D. Support for the router for IPSec

Answer: **D**

Explanation: For AWS Direct Connect, you require:

- VLAN encapsulation
- Port speed and full duplex
- Support for the router for BGP
- BFD configuration
- The network must use single mode Fiber (LX 1Gb and LR 10Gb)

404- An organization has a three-tier application. During peak hours, the private application layer sends 20 Gbps of data per second to and from Amazon S3. Transferring of data is done via NAT gateways that are placed in two subnets. Now, the organization wants the instances in private layer to get software patches from the third party. How should the architecture be designed to meet this requirement?

A. By adding a VPN connection for better throughput

B. By adding an Internet gateway for better throughput

C. By adding a VPC endpoint

D. By adding another NAT gateway

Answer: **C**

Explanation: Amazon VPC endpoints allow you to connect your VPC privately with other AWS services powered by Private Link without an internet gateway or via a NAT instance, VPN, or AWS Direct Connect connection. Instances within your VPC private subnet do not require public IPs to communicate with resources in the service. Multiple endpoints can also be created for a single service.

405- You have AWS Direct Connect connection along with public VIF. Now, you are afraid of loopholes with public VIF. What could be your concern?

A. An EC2 instance with a private IP has a chance of reaching you via the public VIF

B. Your VPC is exposed via the public VIF

C. An EC2 Instance with a public IP has a chance of reaching you via the public VIF

D. Your VPC is exposed to the internet

Answer: C

Explanation: Public VIF connects you to public AWS services. Public IPs get advertised and reachable via Public VIF.

406- You are a Cloud Engineer in an organization, and your CEO wants you to test workspaces for accounts. So, you allocate a set of a workstation with static IPs and desire that only these IPs are accessible to Amazon Workspaces. How will you do this?

   A. By specifying the IP addresses in the Security Group
   B. By specifying the IP addresses in the NACL
   C. By placing a WAF in front of Amazon Workspaces
   D. By creating an IP access control group

Answer: D

Explanation: IP access control group is used to control IP addresses from where users are allowed to access the workspaces. IP access control group act as a firewall, and you can link up to 25 IP access control groups to each directory.

407- An organization is using ALB with various targets behind it, but still, clients are not able to connect to ALB because of whitelisting. How will you, being in the security department, modify the architecture?

   A. By placing a Network Load balancer behind the ALB
   B. By placing a Network Load balancer in front of the ALB
   C. By assigning an Elastic IP to the Application Load Balancer
   D. By assigning a public IP to the Application Load Balancer

Answer: B

Explanation: As ALB IP address keeps changing. In order to avoid this, place Network Load Balancer in front of ALB and assign elastic IP.

408- An organization is using NAT instances for traffic flow in private subnet instances, but now it wants to increase bandwidth and for that, they need to use NAT gateways. How can they automate the provision?

   A. By using AWS Inspector to replace the NAT instances with NAT gateways

B. By using CloudFormation templates to replace the NAT instances with NAT gateways

C. By using OpsWorks to replace the NAT instances with NAT gateways

D. By using AWS Config to change the configuration of the NAT instance to a NAT gateway

Answer: **B**

Explanation: Use a CloudFormation template in order to automate the process of replacing NAT instances with NAT gateway.

409- A company has a VPC for which VPC Flow logs are set up for instances with ENI in the subnet but it shows an error. Why is this error occurring?

"2 123456789911 eni-abc123de 172.31.9.69 172.31.9.12 49761 3389 6 20 4249 1418530010 1418530070 REJECT OK"

A. A request was made on port 443 to the Instance

B. Someone was trying to log into the Instance via RDP

C. Someone was trying to log into the Instance via SSH

D. A request was made on port 80 to the Instance

Answer: **B**

Explanation: The error given in question indicates that someone is trying to log in to the instance via RDP as an error in port 3389 is indicated, which means that it is using RDP protocol.

410- A company has a VPC and subnets in AWS. All subnets in VPC are IPv6 based, and you added a route in the table for CIDR 0.0.0.0/0, but still, communication across all host is not achieved, why?

A. You need to add the default route of 172.132.0.0/16 to the Route table

B. You need to add a route for ::/0 to the route table as well

C. You need to remove the route of 0.0.0.0/0 and add the route of ::/0 instead to allow all communication

D. You need to ensure that the route of 0.0.0.0/0 is removed and a more specific route is placed

Answer: **B**

Explanation: 0.0.0.0/0 is destination CIDR for IPv4 address while with IPv6 addresses, you need to add a route ::/0 in the route table.

411- You have a VPC with EC2 instances hosted in it but it is possible for DDoS attacks to occur on the instances. How would you, as a network design engineer, define a solution to mitigate that attack if any IP address receives a burst of requests?

    A. By using AWS Config to get the IP addresses accessing the EC2 instances
    B. By using AWS Trusted Advisor to get the IP addresses accessing the EC2 instances
    C. By using VPC Flow Logs to get the IP addresses accessing the EC2 instances
    D. By using AWS CloudTrail to get the IP addresses accessing the EC2 instances

Answer: **C**

Explanation: By using VPC Flow Logs, you can identify which IP address sends a burst request to the instances, as VPC Flow Logs show the list of IP addresses that hit instances.

412- An organization stored files in S3 bucket and wants that its clients are able to access these files all over the world with minimal latency. Clients should also able to access the distribution through the domain name. How can this be done?

    A. By creating a resource record in a hosted zone and also creating a PTR record
    B. By creating a resource record in a hosted zone and also creating an ALIAS record
    C. By creating a web-based distribution in CloudFront
    D. By creating an application load balancer and pointing it to the S3 bucket

Answer: **B & C**

Explanation: For accessing the web content with low latency, use CloudFront distribution and as the organization wants to access distribution via its own domain name, use Route 53 with Alias record pointing at CloudFront distribution.

An alias record is a Route 53 extension to DNS. It's similar to a CNAME record, but you can create an alias record both for the root domain and for subdomains. When Route 53 receives a DNS query that matches the name and type of an alias record, Route 53 responds with the domain name that is associated with your distribution.

413- Michael is using EC2 instances with Classic Load Balancer, but when he tries connecting to ELB DNS, he is not getting a response from instances. What are the steps that need to be taken to overcome this issue? (Choose 2)

A. Ensure the Security group for the Load Balancer accepts traffic on port 80 from 0.0.0.0/0
B. Ensure the Security group for the Load Balancer allows traffic on port 80 from 10.0.0.0/16
C. Ensure the Load Balancer is created in the private subnet
D. Ensure the Load Balancer is created in the public subnet

Answer: **A & D**
Explanation: If ELB is not responding when it is internet facing, then it may be that the ELB is in private subnet or SG does not allow the traffic. So, place ELB in a public subnet and allow appropriate rule in SG.

414- If you have a VPC with subnets and instances and you want to move one instance from one subnet to another subnet within the same AZ. Then how would you achieve this?

A. By assigning a new public IP address that pertains to the new subnet and then assigning it to the instance
B. By assigning a new private IP address that pertains to the new subnet and then assigning it to the instance
C. By creating an ENI in the new subnet and attaching it to the instance
D. By creating an AMI out of the EC2 Instance and launching a new instance from the AMI in the new subnet

Answer: **D**
Explanation: If you want to move your instance into another VPC, Region or AZ, then you must create AMI of that instance and then create an instance from this AMI into your desired AZ or region or VPC. Now after creating this, reassign the Elastic IP from the previous instance to the new one.

415- A company has VPC with instances that have public IPs. Now, these instances need to reach web server via port 443 but are unable to do so. The company has already checked that IGW is assigned, route table has a route to IGW, NACL allows outgoing traffic for 443 port and incoming for the ephemeral port. SG allows outbound traffic for port 443 but is still not able to reach web server. What might be the reason behind this issue?

A. The external web server is blocking the requests
B. The Security Group should allow Inbound traffic for port 443
C. The route table should have a route for 10.0.0.0/16 to the Internet gateway

D. You should not use the internet gateway, instead use a NAT gateway for the routing of traffic

Answer: **A**

Explanation: Settings for reaching out the web server is right, so the only issue causing this is at the web server side blocking the request.

416-   An organization has services inside VPC, and they want to give access to its client on these services via mobile devices and tablet. How should they design the architecture?

    A. By using an AWS Managed Direct Connect gateway

    B. By using an AWS Managed Direct Connect connection

    C. By using an AWS Managed VPN

    D. By using a custom VPN server hosted on an EC2 instance

Answer: **D**

Explanation: For connecting a single client to VPC, you need to use customer VPN server hosted on EC2 instance that leverages an internal remote user database. The client is liable for the management of remote access software, including user management, setup, patches and upgrades, as with the VPN software options.

Furthermore, this design brings a possible failure point into the network architecture as a remote access server operates on a single Amazon EC2 instance

417-   You have VPCs in AWS that need to connect to your on-premises network via VPN. You want all traffic to flow via VPC security from the on-premises network. How would you design an architecture for this? (Choose 2)

    A.   By creating a VPC peering connection between the Security VPC and all other VPCs

    B. By creating a VPN connection between the on-premises environment and the Security VPC

    C. By creating a VPN connection between the Security VPC to all other VPCs

    D. By creating a VPN connection between the on-premises environment to all other VPCs

Answer: **B & C**

Explanation: For the given requirement, you need to create a VPN connection between Security VPC and on-premises and Security VPC to other VPCs.

418- If an organization has AWS Direct Connect connection in one region and wants to extend this connection to another AWS region, then how would this be done?

    A. By using an IPSec VPN
    B. By creating a private VIF using the current connection
    C. By using of the Direct Connect gateway
    D. By creating another AWS Direct Connect connection in us-west

Answer: **C**

Explanation: For connecting your AWS Direct Connect connection over a virtual private interface to multiple VPCs in the same or different region, first, create Direct Connect gateway with a virtual private gateway for VPC then create a virtual private interface for AWS Direct Connect connection to Direct Connect gateway.

419- How can you identify the cost of VPN connection or in other words, which factor in VPN is responsible for the costing?

    A. VPG Transfer Out
    B. Data Transfer In
    C. VPN Connection Hours
    D. Data Transfer In

Answer: **C**

Explanation: VPN pricing depends on connection hours. $0.05 per VPN connection-hours, $0.048 per VPN connection-hours for Tokyo and Alaska region and $0.065 per VPN connection-hour for AWS Govcloud US region.

420- An organization has Direct Connect connections and VPN connections as follows:

- Site A VPN 10.2.0.0/24 AS 65000 65000
- Site B VPN 10.2.0.128/18 AS 65000
- Site C DX 10.0.0.0/30 AS 65000 65000
- Site D DX 10.0.0.0/16 AS 65000 65000 65000

Now from the following option, which site would AWS use to reach into the network?

    A. Site C

B. Site B

C. Site A

D. Site D

Answer: **A**

Explanation: As per order of preference, the site with the lowest prefix will be chosen by AWS for a route into the network, and site C is with the lowest prefix.

421- A company wants its VPC network to support speed up to 20Gbps. How can this be made possible? (Choose 2)

A. By placing the instances in a placement group

B. By creating an instance from an instance type that supports the Intel 82599 VF interface

C. By enabling Enhanced Networking if not already done

D. By creating an instance from an instance type that supports Enhanced Networking

Answer: **C & D**

Explanation: By enabling enhanced networking and launching an instance with a type that supports enhanced networking, you can support up to 25 Gbps of speed.

422- An organization wants to create AWS Managed Microsoft AD directory. What pre-requisites need to be taken for this?

A. A NAT gateway in the public subnet

B. The opening of several ports including port 53

C. Usage of a NAT Instance in the VPC

D. A VPC with 2 subnets

Answer: **B & D**

Explanation: For AWS Managed Microsoft AD, you need at least two subnets in VPC in separate AZ. Also, multiple ports need to be open:

- TCP/UDP 53 - DNS
- TCP/UDP 88 - Kerberos authentication
- UDP 123 - NTP
- TCP 135 - RPC
- UDP 137-138 - Netlogon

- TCP 139 - Netlogon
- TCP/UDP 389 - LDAP
- TCP/UDP 445 - SMB
- TCP 636 - LDAPS (LDAP over TLS/SSL)
- TCP 873 - Rsync
- TCP 3268 - Global Catalog
- TCP/UDP 1024-65535 - Ephemeral ports for RPC

423- A company uses EC2 instances in AWS for its application. All the updates and software installation are IPv6 but when they are trying to access software via IPv6 port 80, they cannot access it. What could be the issue behind this?

    A. The egress-only internet gateway needs to be added

    B. The inbound rule to the security group that allows inbound traffic on port 80 for 0.0.0.0/0 needs to be added

    C. The internet gateway for the instance needs to be added

    D. The inbound rule to your security group that allows inbound traffic on port 80 for ::/0 needs to be added

Answer: **D**

Explanation: For IPv6 address, you need to add a port with::/0 in the security group.

424- An educational institute has a VPC and an on-premises location. It also has AWS Direct Connect connection and wants to move its on-premises data into VPC in a secure way so that data confidentiality and integrity is not disturbed. How can this be done? (Choose 3)

    A. By creating an IPSec tunnel between the customer gateway and the Virtual Private Gateway

    B. By attaching a Virtual Private Gateway to the VPC

    C. By setting up a public VIF using the AWS Direct Connect connection

    D. By setting up a private VIF using the AWS Direct Connect connection

Answer: **A, B, & C**

Explanation: Use of AWS Direct Connect connection is faster as compared to VPN so for AWS Direct Connect connection, first, configure a private virtual interface then attach VPG to VPC

and CGW to the on-premises end and then by using IPSec tunnel between CGW and VPG, make the connection secure.

425-   An organization wants to use sub 1 Gbps hosted connection. How can it create VIF using this hosted connection?

    A. By raising a support ticket to accept the hosted connection
    B. By accepting the hosted connection in the console
    C. By requesting for an AWS Direct Connect connection via AWS Support
    D. By creating the hosted connection in the console

Answer: **B**

Explanation: If you want to use sub 1 Gbps connection, then create a hosted connection to the partner you took this connection from, and you need to accept that connection via AWS Direct Connect console.

426-   A company has one IP address range for on-premises network and one IP address range for AWS Cloud. Now it wants to create a VPC and a communication between that VPC and an on-premises network. How do you, as a network design engineer, design this architecture?

    A. By establishing a VPN connection using your Virtual Private Gateway and ensuring that a route is present in your on-premises router to route traffic via the Virtual Private Gateway
    B. By establishing a VPN connection using your customer gateway and ensuring that a route is present in your on-premises router to route traffic via the customer gateway
    C. By setting up a VPC with an address range assigned to cloud
    D. By setting up a VPC with an address range assigned to on premises

Answer: **B & D**

Explanation: As the IP address range has been assigned, then from that IP address, create a VPC. For communication between VPC and on-premises network, use VPN connection using CGW with the appropriate route defined on the on-premises route.

427-   When an organization is using AWS Direct Connect connection and public VIF, then how can it control the advertising of routes?

A. By using MED
B. By using BGP Communities
C. By using BGP Header
D. By using AS_PATH Prepending

Answer: **B**

Explanation: As AWS Direct Connect uses BGP community tags to control the route preference of traffic. In tag, you must define how far you want to propagate prefixes in a network.

These are different prefixes:

- 7224:9100—Local AWS Region
- 7224:9200—All AWS Regions for a continent (for example, North America–wide)
- 7224:9300—Global (all public AWS Regions)

428- A company has its service hosted in private subnet of VPC. Now, it wants to give access of this service to its multiple users. How can this be done?

A. By creating a Network Load Balancer and providing the DNS name to your clients
B. By creating an Application Load Balancer and providing the DNS name to your clients
C. By creating a VPC Interface Endpoint
D. By creating a VPC Endpoint gateway for your service

Answer: **C**

Explanation: VPC interface endpoint is a private link that allows you to connect to the services provided by AWS. These endpoints are created inside VPC via ENI or IP address of the subnet. This private link is powered via private IP. So, this endpoint is accessed from on-premises via AWS Direct Connect.

429- A CloudFront distribution uses S3 as origin, how can you add a security header to the response before it can be relayed back to the client?

A. By creating an OAI for the CloudFront distribution
B. By making sure that the Viewer protocol is set to HTTPS
C. By creating a Lambda function that will run on the edge
D. By changing the Behavior of the origin and setting the configuration for adding the security header

Answer: C

Explanation: By using Lambda Edge, you can execute a Lambda function at an Amazon CloudFront Edge Location. This capability enables intelligent processing of HTTP requests at locations that are close (for the purposes of latency) to your customers. Security headers are a set of headers from a server in the HTTP response to show your browser how to handle the information of your site. For instance, X-XSS-Protection is a header that Internet Explorer and Chrome use to prevent loading websites when attacking cross-site scripting (XSS).

https://aws.amazon.com/blogs/networking-and-content-delivery/adding-http-security-headers-using-lambdaedge-and-amazon-cloudfront/

430-   From the following options, which option is not needed to be set up during configuration of Public VIF for AWS Direct Connect?

    A. Virtual Private Gateway
    B. BGP ASN
    C. VLAN ID
    D. Route Peer IP

Answer: A

Explanation: VPGW is needed for private VIF, so this option is not needed in configuring a public VIF. During configuring of public VIF, you need to define connection router, VLAN ID and BGP ASN.

431-   An organization has a VPC and two on-premises networks. VPC is connected to site A via VPN connection, while being connected to Site B via Direct Connect connection. Now that the route advertised by both CGWs is 10.0.0.0/15, how would the flow of traffic occur from on-premises to AWS?

    A. Traffic will not flow due to the conflict in routes
    B. The traffic will flow primarily through the Internet
    C. The traffic will flow primarily through site B Customer device
    D. The traffic will flow primarily through site A Customer gateway

Answer: C

Explanation: In AWS, by default, Direct Connect path is preferred to send the traffic. It uses Site B primarily as it uses AWS Direct Connect connection for connection between AWS and on premises.

432- If you want to use a VPN for which you have to setup Active-Passive configuration, how will you achieve this? (Choose 2)

   A. By using different ASN numbers
   B. By using IPSec routing
   C. By using more specific routes
   D. By using AS_PATH prepending

Answer: **C & D**

Explanation: For Active/Passive configuration you need to define more specific routes to send traffic to the appropriate data center. Use AS_PATH prepending so that it makes the route less preferred.

433- You have a management network built on VPC. There is a web server on single VPC instance that allows traffic from the internet as well as backend management. You also want the backend management network interface to receive SSH traffic only from the selected IP range, while internet facing web server to receive traffic from all internet IPs. How is that possible?

   A. This is not possible
   B. The organization should create 2 EC2 instances as this is not possible with one EC2 instance
   C. The organization should create 2 network interfaces, one for the internet traffic and the other for the backend traffic
   D. It is not possible to have 2 IP addresses for a single instance

Answer: **C**

Explanation: The network interface is for instances that are in VPC, so create two networks interfaces one for backend and other for internet traffic.

434-   An organization has a database server that only connects to the internet for downloading patches. Now the organization wants to download patches without connecting to the internet. How can this requirement be achieved?

   A.   By setting up the database in a private subnet that connects to the internet via a NAT instance

   B.   By setting up the database in a local data center and using a private gateway to connect the application to the database

   C.   By setting up the database in a public subnet with a security group that only allows inbound traffic

   D.   By setting up the database in a private subnet with a security group that only allows outbound traffic

Answer: **A**

Explanation: For VPC, place web servers in public subnet while database servers in private subnet. For downloading security patches and updates for instances in the private subnet from the internet, it connects to the NAT instance.

435-   A company is using a static VPN connection with 50 routes in the route table. This VPN connection is between the data center and VPC. How would you add more routes to this table? (Choose 2)

   A.   By deleting static VPN and creating a dynamic VPN
   B.   By adding the route to the route table
   C.   By using BGP for routing
   D.   By increasing the limit on the route table

Answer: **A & C**

Explanation: You can use BGP for routing as it has 100 routes advertising limit. By using dynamic VPN, you can increase routes because static VPN supports 50 routes per route table.

436-   On a subnet, default NACL is setup. As network engineer, what will you use mitigate the attack on EC2 instance in a subnet?

   A.   AWS ec2 change-network-acl-entry
   B.   AWS ec2 rename-network-acl-entry
   C.   AWS ec2 create-network-acl-entry

D. AWS ec2 delete-network-acl-entry

Answer: **D**
Explanation: In default NACL, all traffic is allowed; you need to delete all rule from NACL to block the traffic.

437- An organization has infrastructure on an on-premises and VPC. Now, it needs to connect both networks via IPSec tunnel over the internet. The organization decides to terminate IPSec tunnel on CGW and use VPN gateway. What are the benefits of using IPSec tunnel? (Choose 4)

    A. Data integrity protection across the Internet
    B. Peer identity authentication between VPN gateway and Customer gateway
    C. End-to-end Identity authentication
    D. Protection of data in transit over the internet
    E. End-to-end protection of data in transit
    F. Data encryption across the Internet

Answer: **A, B, D, & F**
Explanation: IPSec tunnel provides many benefits like data integrity, data protection, protection of data in transit, and peer identity authentication.

438- An organization has three VPCs whose instances need to pass traffic between each other. How can this requirement be fulfilled?

    A. By peering the VPCs and enabling transitive peering via the route tables
    B. By peering the VPCs to each other in a full mesh configuration
    C. By peering the VPCs and then contacting AWS support to enable transitive peering
    D. By peering the VPCs; transitive peering is now allowed in AWS

Answer: **B**
Explanation: By configuring the VPCs in mesh configuration, all VPCs' instances can communicate to each other, but VPCs do not have overlap CIDR and are in the same account.

439- A company uses ELB in its architecture, and sets its health check interval of 5 seconds with five healthy thresholds and six unhealthy thresholds. After what duration, will the instances become healthy?

   A. 30 seconds
   B. 25 seconds
   C. 10 seconds
   D. 5 seconds

Answer: **B**

Explanation: The healthy check interval multiplied by the healthy threshold will give you the total duration after which instances are marked as healthy.

440- An organization wants to launch two instances with optimal performance in each VPCs that are peered together. How can this be done? (Choose 2)

   A. By ensuring that the MTU for the ENI is set to 1500 for the instances
   B. By ensuring that the instance type support enhanced networking
   C. By ensuring that the instances are launched in subnets in different AZs and creating a placement group
   D. By ensuring that the instances are launched in subnets in the same AZ and creating a placement group

Answer: **B & D**

Explanation: Placement group is a logical grouping of instances within single AZ. Via placement group, low network latency and high network throughput is obtained. For enhanced performance, launch an instance that has enhanced networking supporting.

441- From the following options, which option is incorrect about public IP address?

   A. You can manually associate or disassociate a public IP address
   B. The Public IP allows the instance to be reachable from the internet
   C. When an IP is disassociated from the instance, it is added back to the pool
   D. A public IP address is assigned from Amazon's pool of public IP addresses

Answer: **A**

Explanation: Association of the public IP address is done by AWS from its poll, and when it disassociates from the instance, it will go back to AWS pool again. With this Public IP, an internet reachability is allowed for the instance.

So, you cannot manually associate or disassociate public IP address.

442- An organization has its data center, application, and infrastructure, which it wants to move to AWS. The existing infrastructure has a small amount of legacy application that does not work on AWS. How can the organization migrate the legacy application to AWS?

A. By convincing the client to look for another solution by de-commissioning these applications and seeking out new ones that will run on AWS

B. By creating a hybrid cloud and configuring a VPN tunnel to the on-premises location of the data centre

C. By moving the legacy applications onto AWS first, before you build any infrastructure. Surely, there is an AWS Machine Image that can run this legacy application

D. By creating two VPCs. One containing all the legacy applications and the other containing all the other applications, making a connection between them with VPC peering

Answer: **B**

Explanation: By using hybrid infrastructure, you can create a VPN connection between on-premises and cloud so that communication from each environment to other is happening.

443- Which feature in AWS Direct Connect provides faster detection time of failure?

A. VPN
B. Peering
C. BFD
D. BGP

Answer: **C**

Explanation: Bidirectional Forwarding Detection (BFD) is a network fault detection protocol that provides fast failure detection times, which facilitates faster re-convergence time for dynamic routing protocols.

444- In AWS, which command should you use to automate the network interface configuration on Linux instances?

    A. ec2-Linux-utils

    B. AWS-Linux-utils

    C. ec2-net-utils

    D. AWS-net-utils

Answer: **C**

Explanation: To automate the configuration of the network interface on Linux instances, you need to install additional scripts by AWS from the following command "ec2-net-utils".

445- An organization has its central server on VPC and wants it to be able to connect to other department servers in other VPCs in the same region. How can the organization accomplish this requirement?

    A. By setting up AWS Direct Connect between the central server VPC and each of the departments' VPCs

    B. By setting up an IPSec Tunnel between the central server VPC and each of the departments' VPCs

    C. By setting up VPC peering between the central server VPC and each of the departments' VPCs

    D. None of the above

Answer: **C**

Explanation: VPC peering is a connection between two VPCs so that traffic routes between them. VPC peering can be done in the same region while belonging to a different account.

446- How does an organization connect its on-premises directory service to AWS?

    A. Any of the below given options are acceptable to use as long as they are configured correctly for 10,000 customers

    B. AD Connector

    C. AWS Directory Service for Microsoft Active Directory (Enterprise Edition)

    D. Simple AD

Answer: **B**

Explanation: By using the AD connector, you can use an on-premises directory with AWS.

447- A company wants to use IDS/IPS in its VPC that is capable of scaling thousands of instances within VPC. How would you, as a network design engineer, design the architecture for this?

A. By configuring each host with an agent that collects all network traffic and sends that traffic to the IDS/IPS platform for inspection

B. By configuring servers running in the VPC using the host-based 'route' commands to send all traffic through the platform to a scalable virtualized IDS/IPS

C. By creating a second VPC and route all traffic from the primary application VPC through the second VPC where the scalable virtualized IDS/IPS platform resides

D. By configuring an instance with monitoring software, and the Elastic Network Interface (ENI) set to promiscuous mode packet sniffing to see all traffic across the VPC

Answer: **A**

Explanation: For IDS/IPS platform, use of an agent is better rather than using route command. By configuring the host with an agent, you can collect all traffic and then forward it to IDS/IPS for analyzing. In AWS, Promiscuous mode is not supported and VPC option is increase overhead.

448- How does an enterprise design a flexible SSL/TLS solution that authenticates HTTPS clients via web server using client certificate authentication? (Choose 2)

A. By configuring web servers as the origins for a CloudFront distribution and using custom SSL certificates on CloudFront distribution

B. By configuring web servers with EIPs, placing the web servers in a Route 53 Record Set and configuring health checks against all web servers

C. By configuring ELB with HTTPS listeners and placing the web servers behind it

D. By configuring ELB with TCP listeners on TCP/443 and placing the web servers behind it

Answer: **B & D**

Explanation: For required conditions of HTTPS client authentication, you can use web server directly with Route 53, and you can use ELB because TLS connection does not terminate on ELB and end instances will handle SSL authentication so place instances behind ELB.

449-   A company has its website hosting on AWS. The website is using EC2, S3, Classic- ELB and CloudFront. What preventives would you as network engineer take to secure this website? (Choose 2)

    A. A WAF on the load balancer

    B. A WAF on your CloudFront distribution

    C. A NACL that blocks all ports to your subnets

    D. A restricted bucket policy on S3

Answer: **B & D**

Explanation: By making bucket restrictive and using WAF for Distribution, you can make the website secure. You can also use WAF with ELB, but it is only supported in Application Load Balancer.

450-   You have a web server hosted on AWS using EC2, S3, CloudFront, and ALB. Now you need to identify the IP addresses that access the website. How will you identify if you do not have access on AWS console and API?

    A. By converting the Application Load Balancer to a Classic Load Balancer

    B. The access logs should already have this information

    C. By adding "X-Forwarded For" to the access logs and viewing the access logs

    D. By using the local metadata on the server to access the logs

Answer: **C**

Explanation: Through X-Forwarded for header request, you can identify the IP address of user when you use ALB. The server access logs only show IP address of ELB not user's address so by using x-forwarder for header requests, you can see the IP address of the user.

451-   An organization has its on-premises network that needs to be connected to AWS in such a way that traffic between them will be encrypted and reliable. On-premises network will be able to access AWS S3 resources. How can this be done? (Choose 2)

    A. By creating a Direct Connect connection with a virtual public interface

    B. By creating a VPN connection

    C. By creating a Direct Connect connection with a hosted virtual interface

    D. By creating a Direct Connect connection with a private virtual interface

Answer: **A & B**

Explanation: Via VPN, you can connect your on-premises and AWS VPC. This will provide encrypted and reliable communication. By using Public VIF with Direct Connect, you can connect to AWS service that is not in VPC like S3, Glacier.

452- A company has three-tier application. Its application layer needs to send 20 Gbps data per second to and from S3 in peak hours. There are two NAT gateways in two subnets for communicating private application layer to S3. Instances get software updates from third-party repository. How would you, as a network design engineer, design this architecture?

    A. By removing the NAT gateway and creating a VPC S3 endpoint that allows higher bandwidth throughput as well as tighter security

    B. NAT gateways support 10 Gbps, and two are running; no changes are required to improve this architecture

    C. By keeping the NAT gateway and creating a VPC S3 endpoint that allows higher bandwidth throughput as well as tighter security

    D. By adding a third to a third subnet to allow an increase in demand as NAT gateways support only 10 Gbps

Answer: **C**

Explanation: By using VPC endpoint, you can allow instances in private subnet to access AWS resources like S3. In this way, you have tighter security and high bandwidth throughput.

453- An organization has an application that needs to be monitored and it also wants to monitor all API calls to this application to identify any suspicious activity. How can this be done? (Select any 2)

    A. By using Amazon CloudTrail

    B. By using Amazon CloudWatch Logs

    C. By using Amazon AWS Config

    D. By using Amazon VPC Flow Logs

Answer: **A & B**

Explanation: AWS CloudTrail is a service that enables your AWS account to be managed, complied with, audited, and analyzed for risks. You can log, track, and maintain your account

activities relating to actions across your AWS infrastructure with CloudTrail. CloudTrail offers event history of your AWS account operation, including AWS SDKs, command line tools and other AWS facilities via the AWS Management Console. The history of events simplifies security analysis, tracking and troubleshooting for resource changes.

You can monitor, store, and access your log files from Amazon Elastic Compute Cloud, AWS CloudTrail, Amazon Route 53 and other source by using of Amazon CloudWatch Logs. The related log information can then be retrieved from CloudWatch Logs.

454- How can you design an architecture for transferring a large amount of data among AWS and on-premises with low latency and high consistency?

A. By creating an IPSec tunnel for private connectivity, which increases network consistency and reduces latency

B. By provisioning a Direct Connect connection to an AWS region using a Direct Connect partner

C. This is not possible

D. By creating a VPN tunnel for private connectivity, which increases network consistency and reduces latency

Answer: **B**

Explanation: By using AWS Direct Connect connection, you can create a dedicated connection between on-premises and AWS with high throughput and low latency network.

455- From the following options, which statement is not valid for VPC routing?

A. Each subnet in a VPC must be associated with a routing table

B. You can create additional custom route tables for your VPC

C. You can delete the main route table with the VPC and replace it with a custom route table

D. The VPC comes with an implicit router

Answer: **C**

Explanation: When VPC is created, it has default route table that cannot be deleted although, you can create custom table by adding additional rules in it. You can modify the main route tables.

456-   How would you provide a solution to minimize the DDoS attacks from social media site? (Choose 3)

A.   By creating processes and capabilities to add and remove rules to the instance OS firewall quickly

B.   By adding alert Amazon CloudWatch to look for high Network in and CPU utilization

C.   By using an Elastic Load Balancer with auto-scaling groups at the web, App and Amazon Relational Database Service (RDS) tiers

D.   By adding multiple Elastic Network Interfaces (ENIs) to each EC2 instance to increase the network bandwidth

E.   By using dedicated instances to ensure that each instance has the maximum performance possible

F.   By using an Amazon CloudFront distribution for both static and dynamic content

Answer: **B, C, & F**

Explanation: To avoid DDoS attack, the best practice is that you design an architecture in which application and web server use ELB with Autoscaling group and RDS as database layer. CloudFront for distribution and monitoring is done via CloudWatch.

https://do.awsstatic.com/whitepapers/DDoS_White_Paper_June2015.pdf

457-   A company wants to connect its on-premises AD Microsoft exchange email server with Simple AD in AWS but is unable to do that. Why?

A.   You need to implement SSL before using Simple AD with Exchange Server

B.   The NACLs are blocking the necessary ports

C.   The firewall is blocking the necessary ports

D.   Simple AD does not work with many Microsoft products

Answer: **D**

Explanation: Simple AD is service provided by Microsoft AD, but it has some restrictions; It does not support AD administrative, power shell, the group managed service account and Microsoft applications, etc.

458-   An organization needs to use WAF in its web server, which of the following AWS service supports WAF? (Choose 2)

A. Application Load Balancer

B. CloudFront

C. Lambda

D. Classic Load Balancer

Answer: **A & B**

Explanation: WAF is supported in AWS by CloudFront and Application Load Balancer.

459   When using VPN, what are the features are available? (Choose 3)

A. VPC Peering

B. Third party software VPN appliance

C. AWS VPN CloudHub

D. AWS Managed VPN

Answer: **B, C, & D**

Explanation: If you are using VPN, you get the following features:

- <u>AWS VPN CloudHub</u>: If more than one remote network is present, then this feature helps you to manage the connection
- <u>AWS Managed VPN</u>: Through this, you have IPsec VPN connection in which VGW provides two VPNs in case of automatic failover
- <u>Third-party Software VPN Appliance</u>: You can create your VPN by using third-party software VPN appliance in VPC

460-   If you have a dynamic VPN connection but you are unable to see routes for the connection, then what could be the reason behind this?

A. You have not set BFD for the connection

B. The route propagation is not set in the Route table

C. The internal firewall is blocking the routes

D. The NACL's are not configured properly

Answer: **B**

Explanation: For dynamic routing, you need to enable route propagation on routing tables. Otherwise, routes will be unable to be viewed in route tables.

461- An institute has its application on AWS and for storage of data, it uses S3 with CloudFront distribution but observes that no data would appear on the application. Even the CloudFront is configured with their domain name cdn.ips.com. What might be the reason?

A. There is no host record created in Route 53 pointing to cdn.ips.com
B. There is no record in Route 53 pointing to cdn.ips.com as the ALIAS
C. Use Elastic Cache to serve images instead of S3
D. Policy has not been set for shared access to the bucket

Answer: **B**

Explanation: For using your own domain, you need to define alias record in Route 53 that points CloudFront. Most probably, there is no Alias record that points to your domain an that is why no data appears.

462- An organization is using EC2 instance inside and outside VPC, and wants the best transmission rate. How would this be achieved? (Choose 2)

A. By configuring the external ENI with an MTU of 1500 and the internal ENI with an MTU of 9001
B. By configuring the single ENI for an MTU transmission rate of 9001
C. By configuring two ENI's for instance, one for internal traffic and the other for external traffic
D. By configuring an ENI for instance for both internal and external traffic

Answer: **A & C**

Explanation: First create two ENIs and then configure the internal ENI with MTU 9001 for internal VPC communication while external ENI with 1500 MTU, which is for huge Ethernet packet size over the internet.

463- An enterprise has some instances that are in stop state, but the enterprise is still charged for this instance. Why?

A. The enterprise has Elastic IPs associated with those instances
B. the enterprise is being charged for the EBS volumes
C. Stored instances incur a charge no matter which state they are in
D. Instances in the stopped state still incur a charge within AWS

Answer: A

Explanation: You are charged for Elastic IP as they are associated with instances that are running. To Elastic IP, only one instance is attached. If you stop or terminate the instance, disassociate that IP from it as it is not used anymore.

464-   From which of the following command can you list the metrics of Direct Connect?

    A. AWS cloudwatch list-metrics --namespace "AWS/DX

    B. AWS cloudwatch list-metrics --namespace "AWS/DC

    C. AWS cloudwatch list-metrics --namespace "AWS/Direct Connect

    D. AWS cloudwatch list-metrics --namespace "AWS/Direct

Answer: A

Explanation: Through this command, you can view all available metrics from Direct Connect.

465-   You want to transfer a large amount of data from on-premises application to AWS VPC. Now you are concerned about the overall transfer costs required for this application. You know that it is potentially not going to deploy a hybrid environment for the customer-facing part of the application that needs to be run in a VPC. Given that, the data transferred to AWS is new every time, what suggestions would you give to the company to help in reducing the overall cost of data transfer to AWS?

    A. Suggest leaving the data required for the application on-premises and using a VPN to query the on-premises database data from EC2 when needed

    B. Suggest using AWS import/export to transfer the TBs of data while synchronizing the new data as it arrives

    C. Suggest provisioning a Direct Connect connection between the on-premises data center and the AWS region

    D. Suggest provisioning a VPN connection between the on-premises data center and the AWS region using the VPN section of a VPC

Answer: C

Explanation: By using AWS Direct Connect connection, you can create a dedicated connection between on-premises and AWS with high throughput and low latency network. The overall cost is also reduced for the network.

466- An organization has a VPC with CIDR 10.0.0.0/24 that supports 256 IP addresses. Now, it wants to split this VPC into two subnets each with 128 IPs. How can the IP addresses be allocated to subnets?

    A. One subnet will use CIDR block 10.0.0.0/25 (for addresses 10.0.0.0 - 10.0.0.127) and the other will use CIDR block 10.0.0.128/25 (for addresses 10.0.0.128 - 10.0.0.255)

    B. This is not possible

    C. One subnet will use CIDR block 10.0.0.0/127 (for addresses 10.0.0.0 - 10.0.0.127) and the other will use CIDR block 10.0.0.128/255 (for addresses 10.0.0.128 - 10.0.0.255)

    D. One subnet will use CIDR block 10.0.0.0/25 (for addresses 10.0.0.0 - 10.0.0.127) and the other will use CIDR block 10.0.1.0/25 (for addresses 10.0.1.0 - 10.0.1.127)

Answer: **A**

Explanation: As VPC CIDR block is 10.0.0.0/24, it has 256 IPs. One subnet with 10.0.0.0/25 and the other with 10.0.0.128/25.

467- An organization wants to use the same set of nameservers for multiple hosted zone in Route 53. How can this be possible?

    A. By importing the domain in Route 53

    B. By creating a Reusable Delegation Set in the console

    C. By creating a Reusable Delegation Set in the API

    D. This is not possible

Answer: **C**

Explanation: Create a delegation set (a group of four name servers) that can be reused by multiple hosted zones. If a hosted zoned ID is specified, CreateReusableDelegationSet marks the delegation set associated with that zone as reusable.

468- An enterprise uses AWS Direct Connect connection, but if it fails, then which backup connection should be used? (Choose 2)

    A. A peering connection

    B. A VPN connection

    C. There is no need to configure this as AWS will fall back to a secondary Direct Connect connection as per SLA

D. A secondary Direct Connect connection

Answer: **B & D**
Explanation: For failover, you can create secondary AWS Direct Connect, or you can use VPN connection. Configure any of the options as a backup.

469- How does an organization create two different VPCs in two different accounts when it also wants to connect both VPCs to central repository?

   A. By creating an OpenVPN instance in central VPC and establishing an IPSec tunnel between VPCs
   B. By creating a Direct Connect connection from each VPC endpoint to the central VPC
   C. By creating a VPC peering connection with the central VPC
   D. By migrating each VPC resources to the central VPC using migration tools such as Import/Export, Snapshot, AMI Copy, and S3 sharing

Answer: **C**
Explanation: By using VPC peering connection between VPCs, you can enable routing of traffic between them so, create VPC peering of both accounts to central VPC.

470- An enterprise is using VPN connection for connecting its on-premises network to AWS. How can it perform the monitoring of the VPN?

   A. AWS Config
   B. AWS CloudWatch
   C. AWS WAF
   D. AWS VPC Flow Logs

Answer: **B**
Explanation: For monitoring of VPN tunnels, you can use AWS CloudWatch that collects and processes the raw data of VPN.

471- An organization is using AWS Workspaces, and needs MFA for this service. Which pre-requisite is required for this?

    A. An MFA Server deployed in AWS and in the on-premises environment

    B. An MFA Server deployed in AWS

    C. A RADIUS Server deployed in the on-premises environment

    D. An MFA Server deployed in the on-premises environment

Answer: **C**

Explanation: To enable MFA for AWS WorkSpaces, you need to deploy Remote Authentication Dial-In User Service (RADIUS) server in your on-premises infrastructure.

472- An institute has a large number of students, and is considering to use AWS Workspaces. The data of students is stored in on-premises AD. How can the institute set up the authentication process so that on-premises AD is used for user authentication? (Choose 2)

    A. By creating a VPN between the datacenter AWS and the on-premise environment

    B. By creating a Direct Connect connection between the datacenter and AWS

    C. By deploying an AD Connector in AWS that will be used to connect to the on-premises AD

    D. By deploying a Hosted AD in AWS that will be used to connect to the on-premises AD

Answer: **B & C**

Explanation: You can use AD Connector to use your on-premises AD. By using Direct Connect, you can create a private connection link between on-premises and AWS.

473- A company has a web server hosted on AWS EC2 instances with a public IP. This IP is mapped to the domain name but after the instance restarts, it is not accessible via domain name. What would be the reason behind this?

    A. The public IP addresses have changed after the instance was stopped and restarted

    B. The public IP addresses need to associated with the ENI again

    C. The network interfaces need to initialized again

    D. The Route 53 hosted zone needs to be restarted

Answer: **A**

Explanation: When instances is restarted after stop, its IP address is changed. So as the previous IP is mapped to the domain, and that is why it becomes inaccessible.

474-   When you create a VPN connection between AWS and on-premises, how many tunnels will you get?

A. 2
B. 3
C. 1
D. 4

Answer: **A**

Explanation: Each VPN connection has 2 tunnels, each with a unique VPG public IP address. In case if one tunnel fails, it goes automatically to the other.

475-   If an organization is using multiple IP addresses on EC2 instances, what are the benefits? (Choose 3)

A. Broadcasting is possible on the subnet
B. Hosts multiple websites on a single server by using multiple SSL certificates
C. Supports multiple network interfaces
D. Failovers to a standby instance

Answer: **B, C, & D**

Explanation: When you assign multiple IP addresses to the instance, you get multiple website hosts using multiple SSL certificates, multiple network interfaces, and failover to standby instance.

476-   From the following options, which statement is wrong with reference to placement groups?

A. You can move an existing instance into a placement group
B. A cluster placement group cannot span multiple Availability Zones
C. A placement group can span over peered VPCs
D. You can merge placement groups

Answer: D

Explanation: In the placement group you cannot merge the placement group, you can span it over peered VPCs, move the existing instance to it, or use placement group with two types of cluster and spread.

477- When using BGP route, what is the limit of BGP advertised routes per route table?

    A. 200

    B. 100

    C. 50

    D. 10

Answer: B

Explanation: You have a limit of 100 routes when using BGP.

478- Which encryption standard is used in a VPN connection?

    A. Blowfish

    B. Twofish

    C. TripleDES

    D. AES

Answer: D

Explanation: The recommended encryption protocols for VPN are AES 128/256, SHA 1/256 and DH groups.

479- An organization needs to stop IPv6 connection of resources from the internet to instances in public subnets. How would this be done?

    A. NAT gateway

    B. ingress-only Internet gateway

    C. egress-only Internet gateway

    D. Internet gateway

Answer: C

Explanation: When you use Egress only internet gateway, it restricts IPv6 communications generating from the internet to instances while it allows instance to internet communications.

480- You have three VPCs and you want to communicate in such a way that VPC A and VPC B should be accessible from VPC C. How would you do this?

  A. By creating VPC peering from VPC C and adding a route to VPC A peering connection
  B. By creating VPC peering from VPC C and adding a route to VPC B peering connection
  C. Not possible
  D. By creating VPC peering from VPC A and adding a route to VPC B peering connection

Answer: **A & B**

Explanation: VPC peering is only possible from VPC C to VPC B and from VPC C to VPC A as you want to access VPC A and VPC B from VPC C. Routes are also required to be added in both VPCs in the peering connection.

481- An organization has a large number of EC2 instances running in a placement group that are all performing well. However, when the organization tries to add new instances in the group, it receives capacity error. How can this issue be resolved?

  A. By making sure all that the instances are of the same size and then trying the launch again
  B. By requesting a capacity increase from AWS as you are initially limited to 10 instances per Placement Group
  C. By stopping and restarting the instances in the Placement Group and then trying the launch again
  D. By making a new Placement Group and launching the new instances in the new group, and also making sure that the Placement Groups are in the same subnet

Answer: **C**

Explanation: If you get a capacity error, then try to relaunch the instance after some duration or submit a new request with a reduced number of launching instances. Try to launch a new instance with different instance type or not defining any specific AZ.

482- Which AWS service can you use to host AD data in the cloud that does not support all features and does not need to be used with Workspaces?

    A. AD server on a large EC2 instance
    B. Hosted Microsoft AD
    C. AD Connector
    D. Simple AD service

Answer: **D**

Explanation: Simple AD is service provided by Microsoft AD to manage and connect to EC2 instances and user accounts, provide SSO and group memberships, as well as create and apply group policy.

483- As a network engineer, how can you make one VPN to be preferred over another?

    A. By using BGP priority
    B. By using AS-path prepending
    C. By using less specific routes
    D. By using more specific routes

Answer: **D**

Explanation: By using more specific routes to send traffic, you can make one VPN more preferable over another.

484- An enterprise has its main document server VPC in AWS on which it only wants to give access to its premium customers. All customers have their own VPCs on AWS. They also want that none of the customers' VPC gets to access each other. How can they achieve this?

    A. By setting up all the VPCs with the same CIDR but having your company's VPC as a centralized VPC
    B. By setting up VPC peering between your company's VPC and each of the clients' VPC. Each client should have VPC peering set up between each other to speed up access time
    C. By setting up VPC peering between your company's VPC and each of the clients' VPCs
    D. By setting up VPC peering between your company's VPC and each of the clients' VPCs but blocking the IPs from CIDR of the clients' VPCs to deny them access to each other

Answer: **C**

Explanation: VPC peering is a connection between two VPCs so that traffic routes between them. VPC peering can be done in the same region but belongs to a different account. So create VPC peering between company VPCs and client VPCs.

485- Which origin protocol policy in CloudFront is used to allow communication with origin through HTTP/HTTPS?

   A. Match viewer
   B. HTTP
   C. HTTPS
   D. None of these

Answer: **A**

Explanation: Match viewer is origin protocol policy that can be used to allow both HTTP/HTTPS communication with origin.

486- Which protocol is used for dynamic routing in VPN connections?

   A. TCP
   B. ICMP
   C. BGP
   D. UDP

Answer: **C**

Explanation: For dynamic routing in VPN connection, you can use BGP that exchanges the information among CGW and VPG.

487- An enterprise has link aggregation group to AWS that uses two 1 Gbps connections, and now it wants to maximize the throughput on this link. How can this be done?

   A. By adding three 1 Gbps connections to the Link Aggregation Group
   B. By adding two 1 Gbps connections to the Link Aggregation Group
   C. By adding two 10 Gbps connections to the Link Aggregation Group
   D. By adding one 10 Gbps connection to the Link Aggregation Group

Answer: B

Explanation: When you are creating a Link Aggregation Group (LAG), there are some rules like:

- All connections support 1 Gbps or 10 Gbps
- Maximum 4 connection is allowed
- All connections run at the same AWS Direct Connect endpoints

488- A company is using EC2 instance to host a web server. The instance is in VPC with public and private ENIs. This instance is connected to the RDS instance. The VPC has two subnets; in one, backup is managed. When the ENI is moved from the previous instance to backup instance, the company notices that it is unable to access the database server from the web server. What would be the issue behind this?

    A. It is not possible to move ENIs across subnets. Hence, the move operation would fail

    B. The instance needs to be restarted so that it can start using the ENI

    C. The security group for the database is blocking the connection to the web server in the new subnet

    D. The database server needs to get a new public IP to work with the ENI

Answer: C

Explanation: When an ENI move from one subnet to another, then the private IP of the ENI will change to reflect the IP of the new subnet so that SG allows traffic from the private IP of the original one. You need to modify the SG of DB to allow access.

489- From the following options, which one is true regarding the configuration of HTTPS in CloudFront for S3 origin? (Choose 3)

    A. If you require HTTPS for communication between CloudFront and Amazon S3, you must change the value of Viewer Protocol Policy to Redirect HTTP to HTTPS or HTTPS Only

    B. Even if an S3 bucket is configured as a website endpoint, https can be used between CloudFront and S3

    C. CloudFront always forwards requests to S3 by using the protocol that viewers used to submit the requests

    D. Amazon S3 provides the SSL/TLS certificate

Answer: A, C, & D

Explanation: If you configure S3 bucket as the website endpoint, then you will not be able to set CloudFront with S3 using HTTPS communication because S3 does not support HTTPS connections. From the given option, all the other three is correct while option B is incorrect. S3 provides SSL/TLS certificate. If S3 is the origin, then CloudFront sends the request to S3 via protocol. You need to alter the value of the Viewer Protocol Policy to Redirect HTTP to HTTPS or HTTPS only if you want HTTPS to communicate between CloudFront and AmazonS3.

490- From the following commands, which command is used to get public IP of an instance when it is in running the state?

   A. curl http://10.0.1.0/latest/meta-data/public-ipv4
   B. curl http://169.254.169.254/latest/meta-data/public-ipv4
   C. curl http://127.0.0.1/latest/meta-data/public-ipv4
   D. curl http://254.169.254.169/latest/meta-data/public-ipv4

Answer: **D**

Explanation: By using this command, you get the following information.

- ami-id
- ami-launch-index
- ami-manifest-path
- local-ipv4 etc.

491- When an organization is using Elastic IP, then in what situation will they be charged?

   A. When you have dissociated the Elastic IP address
   B. When Elastic IP is associated with a stopped instance
   C. When the instance has only one Elastic IP address attached to it
   D. When the Elastic IP is associated with a running instance

Answer: **C & D**

Explanation: You charged for Elastic IP as they are associated with instances. Instances associated with the Elastic IP address are always running and only one instance is attached to it.

492- A company is using a VPN connection, and they are considering to use jumbo frames for larger network packets across the VPN. What is your recommendation as a network engineer for this situation?

    A. You disagree on this since using jumbo frames is not possible in AWS

    B. You disagree on this, since using jumbo frames could slow down the traffic

    C. You agree on this, but also make the suggestion to use larger instance types on the AWS side

    D. You agree on this, since it would definitely help in sending more data across the VPN connection

Answer: **B**

Explanation: Jumbo frames should be used with caution for internet-bound traffic or any traffic that leaves a VPC. Packets are fragmented by intermediate systems, which slows down this traffic. Jumbo frames allow more than 1500 bytes of data by increasing the payload size for a packet and thereby increasing the overhead packet percentage.

493- From the following options, which network mask is capable of hosting 1000 address in a newly created subnet?

    A. /22

    B. /32

    C. /30

    D. /21

Answer: **A**

Explanation: The network mask /22 has the capability to host 1022 hosts in a network.

494- How will you identify the instance subnet, SG, and VPC from the following commands?

    A. By using the command AWS ec2 describe-network-acl

    B. By using the command AWS ec2 describe-instances

    C. By using the command AWS ec2 describe-security-groups

    D. By using the command AWS vpc describe-all

Answer: **B**

Explanation: By using this command, you can identify the subnet, VPC, and SG associated with that instance.

495- From the following options, which one is not right for NAT gateways?

   A. A NAT gateway supports the TCP and UDP protocol
   B. You can associate a security group with a NAT gateway
   C. You can associate exactly one Elastic IP address with a NAT gateway
   D. A NAT gateway supports bursts of up to 10 Gbps of bandwidth

Answer: **B**
Explanation: NAT gateways support up to 10 Gbps of bandwidth. You can associate one Elastic IP address to it but you cannot associate an SG to NAT gateway. Although, you can use SG for instances in private subnets.

496- An organization has its application hosted on EC2 instance in an AWS but faced some issues, and for that, it needs to monitor the network packets. How would this be done?

   A. By using CloudWatch metric
   B. By using another instance then setting up a port to "promiscuous mode" and sniffing the traffic to analyze the packets
   C. By using a network monitoring tool provided by an AWS partner
   D. By using the VPC Flow Logs

Answer: **C**
Explanation: To monitor or capture actual network packets, you need to use network monitoring tools provided by AWS partners. Some partners provide firewall appliances place in gateway for outgoing and incoming traffic.

497- You have AWS cloud environment, and you want to monitor the changes that occur in the environment as well as the traffic flow of that environment. How would you do this? (Choose 2)

   A. By configuring an IPS/IDS systems such as Palo Alto Network that monitors, filters, and alerts users of all potential hazardous traffic leaving the VPC

B. By configuring an IPS/IDS system, such as Palo Alto Networks and using a promiscuous mode that monitors, filters, and alerts of all potential hazardous traffic leaving the VPC

C. By configuring an IPS/IDS in promiscuous mode, which will listen to all packet traffic and API changes

D. By configuring an IPS/IDS to listen and block all suspected bad traffic coming into and out of the VPC. Also, configure CloudTrail with CloudWatch Logs to monitor all changes within an environment

Answer: **A & D**

Explanation: Promiscuous mode is not supported by AWS, so the other two options are automatically incorrect. For monitoring the changes in environment, you can use CloudTrail and CloudWatch metric while IDS and IPS are used for traffic monitoring of network and alert about any occurring issue that affect the traffic.

498- An organization has a VPC CIDR 10.0.0.0/20 and now it wants to create a subnet from the same CIDR block of VPC. What is the maximum number, and the minimum number of IP addresses that are allowed by VPC as we all know that allowed block sizes are between /28 netmask and /16 netmask?

A. The maximum is 65,536 and the minimum is 16. The created VPC supports 4096 IP addresses

B. Maximum is 65,536 and the minimum is 24. The created VPC supports 28 IP addresses

C. Maximum is 256 and the minimum is 16. The created VPC supports 24 IP addresses

D. Maximum is 28 and the minimum is 16. The created VPC supports 24 IP addresses

Answer: **A**

Explanation: /16 netmask allows 65,536 IP addresses while /28 netmask allows 16 IP addresses. In the question given, there is /20 which means it gives 4096 IP addresses.

32-20= 12 so 2^12=4096 IP addresses

499- How, in AWS, do you configure high availability for VPN connection? (Choose 2)

A. By configuring Direct Connect

B. By configuring Dynamic Routing

C. By configuring Static Routing

D. By configuring Redundant Customer Gateways

Answer: **B & D**

Explanation: VPN is configured for connecting VPC to remote data centers easily and quickly for high availability. You can use dynamic routing for automatic failover and for using more CGW as well.

500- A company has its legacy application hosted on an EC2 instance that is tied to a license MAC address but whenever the instance restarts, it loses the MAC address. What would you do to avoid this?

    A. Use a VPC with an elastic network interface that has a fixed MAC Address

    B. Use a VPC with a private subnet and configure the MAC address to be tied to that subnet

    C. Use a VPC with a private subnet for the license and a public subnet for the EC2

    D. Make sure any EC2 instance that you deploy has a static IP address mapped to the MAC address

Answer: **A**

Explanation: By using ENI, you can maintain the private IP, Elastic IP and MAC address of an instance. By using VPC with ENI, if instance restarts, it will not change the MAC address.

501- An organization has 100 Mbps line and wants to use a Direct Connect connection. How would this be done?

    A. By contacting an AWS Partner for this requirement

    B. This is possible only if you upgrade to a 500 Mbps line

    C. This is possible only if you upgrade to a 200 Mbps line

    D. This is not possible with a 100 Mbps line

Answer: **A**

Explanation: 1 Gbps and 10 Gbps is available for 50, 100, 200, 300, 400 and 500 Mbps. You can order from AWS partners that support AWS Direct Connect.

502- A company establishes AWS Direct Connect connection between AWS and its on-premises network via 1 GB Ethernet connection. Everything is verified and correct but it is still incompetent to work as per expectation. Why?

    A. The connections have support for 802.1Q VLANs, which is an issue
    B. Auto-Negotiation for the port is not disabled
    C. The connection must be 10 GBs or greater
    D. Your network supports BGP, which is an issue

Answer: **B**

Explanation: For AWS Direct Connect connection, there are some requirements:

- Auto-negotiation for port must be disabled
- Connection require single-mode fiber for 1 Giga bit or 10 Gigabit
- Network supports BGP and BGP MD5 authentication
- 802.1Q VLANs must be supported across the connections

503- A company has two connections, i.e., AWS Direct Connect and VPN connections. After setting all data, traffic preferred VPN connection rather than Direct Connect. For VPN connection, a longer AS_PATH is prepended. As a Network Engineer, how would you make AWS Direct Connect the preferable connection for traffic?

    A. By advertising less specific prefixes on the VPN connection
    B. By increasing the MED property on the VPN connection
    C. By reconfiguring the VPN as a static VPN instead of dynamic
    D. By removing the prepended AS_PATH

Answer: **A**

Explanation: For VPN, more specific routes are defined in route tables that are used to route traffic so fewer specific routes are used to make AWS Direct Connect the preferable connection.

504- A company has two VPCs, both peered together with proper NACL and SG. Route A's route-table is also configured so that traffic flows from A to B but when trying to ping VPC B from VPC A, the company is unable to do that. Why?

    A. The route tables in VPC B have not been configured
    B. NACL does not work in peered VPCs hence, the requests will not work

C. Security Groups do not work in peered VPCs hence, the requests will not work

D. The VPCs have overlapping CIDR blocks

Answer: **A**

Explanation: To send traffic from one instance to another in VPCs peered together, you need to add routes in the route table of both VPCs. In that case, route table of VPC B is not configured and that why it is not pingable.

505- In AWS, which feature of AWS VPN helps you to add VPN routes in route table automatically?

      A. Route Prepending

      B. Route Navigation

      C. Peer Routing

      D. Route Propagation

Answer: **D**

Explanation: For dynamic routing, you need to enable route propagation on routing tables. Otherwise, the route is not shown in route tables. It basically automates the propagation of routes in the route table.

506- An organization needs to aggregate multiple 1-gigabit or 10-gigabit connection at single AWS Direct Connect to assume all of them as a single connection. What should be used to do this?

      A. VPN Connection Peering

      B. Connection Addition Group

      C. Link Aggregation Group

      D. Direct Connection Peering

Answer: **C**

Explanation: Link aggregation group in AWS is a logical interface that uses LA control protocol for aggregation into single AWS Direct Connect.

507- How many minimum subnets are available in DB SG for RDS instance?

    A. 4
    B. 3
    C. 2
    D. 1

Answer: **C**

Explanation: There are two AZs for each DB subnet group in a region. If one primary instance fails, RDS goes to secondary/stand by DB.

508- If an organization wants to enable enhanced networking with ENA, then what pre-requisites are needed to be taken? (Choose 3)

    A. Using Linux version 3.2 or greater
    B. Using an HVM Instance Type
    C. Launching the instance in a VPC
    D. Using a para-virtual Instance Type

Answer: **A, B, & C**

Explanation: To enable enhanced networking with ENA, you need to launch an instance with HVM instance type in VPC. HVM Linux supported version is 3.2 or greater.

509- If you have a web server in AWS and you want to allow HTTP and HTTPS protocols, then for which ports do you configure them on in SG? (Choose 2)

    A. 443
    B. 20
    C. 80
    D. 22

Answer: **A & C**

Explanation: For HTTP, port 80 needs to be allowed while for HTTPS, port 443 needs to be allowed.

About Our Products

Other products from IPSpecialist LTD regarding Cloud Computing are:

- AWS Certified Cloud Practitioner Technology Workbook
- AWS Certified Solutions Architect - Associate Workbook
- AWS Certified Developer - Associate Technology Workbook
- AWS Certified SysOps Administrator - Associate Technology Workbook
- AWS Certified DevOps Engineer - Professional Technology Workbook
- AWS Certified Solutions Architect - Professional Technology Workbook
- AWS Certified Advanced Networking – Specialty Technology Workbook
- AWS Certified Big Data – Specialty Technology Workbook
- AWS Certified Security – Specialty Technology Workbook
- Google Certified Associate Cloud Engineer Technology Workbook
- Google Certified Professional Cloud Architect Technology Workbook

Upcoming products from IPSpecialist LTD regarding AWS technology are:

- AWS Certified DevOps Engineer - Professional v2 (Exam Update) Technology Workbook

Note from the Author:

Reviews are gold to authors! If you have enjoyed this book and it has helped you along your certification, would you consider rating and reviewing it?

Made in the USA
Monee, IL
12 June 2022

97900184R00129